COMPLETE

STEM SMART

SCIENCE TECHNOLOGY ENGINEERING MATH

Grade 2

ISBN: 978-1-77149-506-6

Printed in China

Dear Parents and Guardians,

The acronym "**STEM**" stands for "**S**cience, **T**echnology, **E**ngineering, and **M**ath." These four fields of integrated study are essential to children in developing problem-solving and analytical skills needed to be successful in school and in life.

The ***Complete STEM Smart*** series is a set of innovative STEM-based workbooks that covers Grade 1 to Grade 6. Each of these resourceful workbooks comprises four major sections: Life Systems, Structures and Mechanisms, Matter and Energy, and Earth and Space Systems. Each section has two parts: Basic Science Concepts and STEM Experiments.

- Basic Science Concepts – introducing grade-appropriate basic science concepts with correlated units to help children build a strong foundation in science
- STEM Experiments – allowing children to experience hands-on learning to develop logical and critical thinking skills, and to make practical connections among science, technology, engineering, and math

Through using our ***Complete STEM Smart*** workbooks, your child will be encouraged to ask questions, make observations, think critically, and explain his or her reasonings. As your child comes across any obstacles through the experiments, he or she will discover that these obstacles can help make the learning experience positive and valuable and understand that it is the key to success.

Furthermore, "Fun to Know" and our bonus online resources with "Trivia Questions" are provided to inspire and motivate your young scientist, technology specialist, engineer, or mathematician through the STEM journey of discovering this world!

Your Partner in Education,
STEM Team at Popular Book Company (Canada) Ltd.

Table of Contents

Section 1: Life Systems

Basic Science Concepts

STEM Experiments

Basic Science Concepts

STEM Experiments

Basic Science Concepts

STEM Experiments

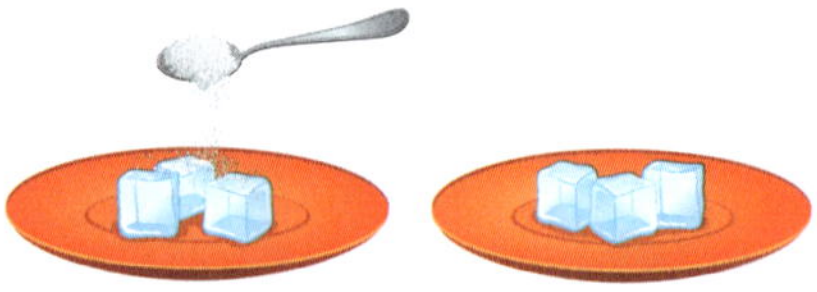

Section 4: Earth and Space Systems

Basic Science Concepts

STEM Experiments

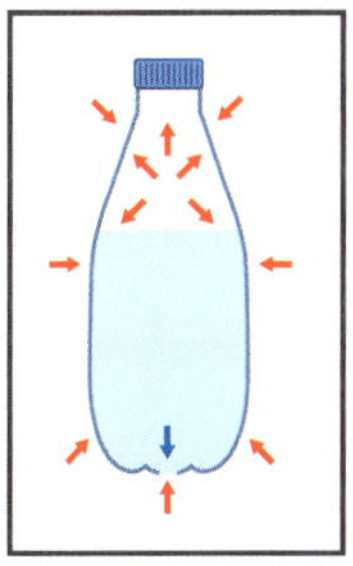

Section 1

Life Systems

1 Animals – Parts of the Body

All animals have body parts with important jobs. Some body parts are similar for many animals. Others look very different. In this unit, you will sort animals by their similarities and differences. You will also look at the functions of major body parts.

After completing this unit, you will

- know the locations and functions of some body parts.
- be able to identify the different body parts and what they are used for.
- know that animal body parts have similarities and differences.

Vocabulary

animals: living things that grow, move, eat, reproduce, and react to the world around them

mammals: animals that have hair, are warm-blooded, and produce milk

Extension

Have you ever wondered why animals have tails? Animals have tails for many reasons, such as for balancing, steering, defending, and attacking. For example, cats use their tails to balance; scorpions use theirs to attack; horses use them to brush away bugs; monkeys use theirs to grasp tree branches; and fish steer with them. In fact, dogs can even use their tails to express their feelings. If a dog's tail is down and wags slowly, the dog might be in fear; when it is happy, its tail tends to wag energetically from side to side.

A. Label the highlighted body parts with the help of the given letters.

B. Identify and check ✔ the body parts each animal has. Then answer the questions.

1.

lizard

Ⓐ legs
Ⓑ wings
Ⓒ a shell
Ⓓ a tail

2.

snail

Ⓐ legs
Ⓑ wings
Ⓒ a shell
Ⓓ a tail

3.

bird

Ⓐ legs
Ⓑ wings
Ⓒ a shell
Ⓓ a tail

4.

mouse

Ⓐ legs
Ⓑ wings
Ⓒ a shell
Ⓓ a tail

5. Name one body part that all of the animals above have. ____________

6. Give an example of an animal that does not have a tail. ____________

7. Give an example of an animal that has a shell. ____________

C. **Identify the animal body part in each picture.**

1.

____

2.

____

3.

____

4.

____

D. **Draw lines to match the functions of each animal's body parts.**

1. duck

eyes •	• to fly
wings •	• to see
feet •	• to walk/swim

2. crab

shell •	• to attack
legs •	• to walk
claws •	• to protect

E. Read the passage. Then answer the questions.

Whales – More Like Us or Fish?

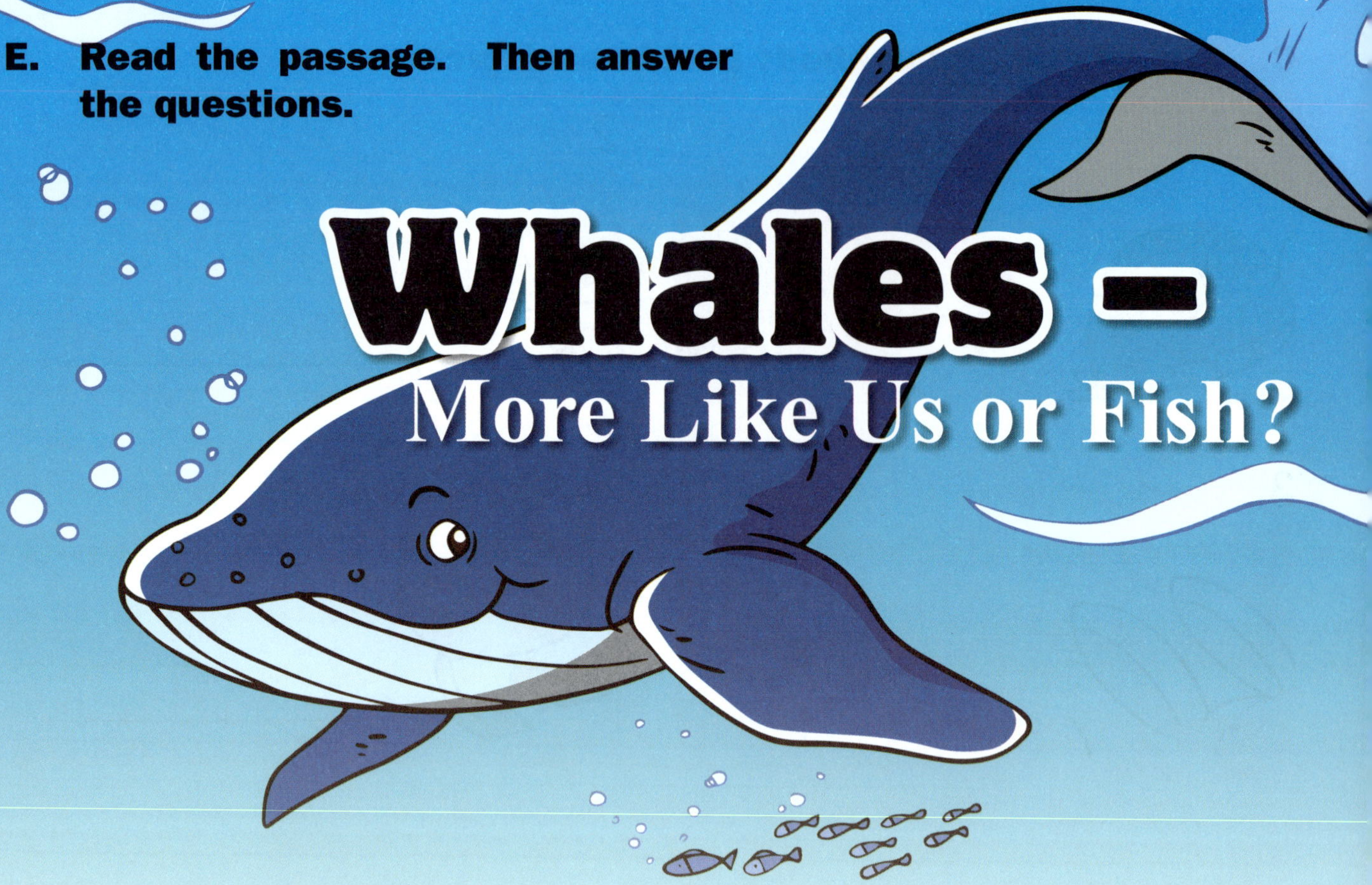

Some people think whales are fish, but they are not. They are mammals like us.

Like people, whales cannot breathe underwater. They rise to the surface to breathe. All whales breathe through blowholes on top of their heads to get air from above the water to their lungs. The puff of mist produced by their exhalation is called "blow." Blowholes are surrounded by muscles that keep the hole closed while underwater and open while above surface.

Unlike people, whales can hold their breath for a very long time. Some whales can spend up to an hour underwater before coming to the surface to breathe. No wonder some people think whales are fish.

1. Write **T** for true and **F** for false.

a. Whales are fish. ____

b. Whales have to rise to the surface of the water to breathe. ____

c. Whales get air to their lungs through their mouths. ____

d. Whales close their blowholes while underwater. ____

e. Some whales can stay underwater for almost an hour in one breath. ____

2. Draw a blowhole for the whale. Then draw the blow that the whale produces to show how it breathes.

2 Animal Characteristics

Scientists classify animals by their physical characteristics. In this unit, you will learn how to classify animals. You will also see how characteristics or behaviors help predators hunt and prey survive.

After completing this unit, you will

- understand what helps predators catch their food.
- understand what helps prey escape from predators.
- be able to classify animals as mammals, birds, fish, reptiles, or amphibians.

Vocabulary

predator: an animal that kills another animal for food

prey: an animal killed by another for food

Extension

Earthworms are important prey for many animals, such as birds and moles. Although earthworms do not have special body parts to defend themselves, they are sensitive to vibrations. Once they feel movements around them, they crawl down quickly to hide themselves in the soil. Also, earthworms have an amazing ability to regenerate their body parts. They can grow new tails if their tails are cut off or eaten by predators.

Go outside to observe the natural world and discover more about predator-prey relationships.

A. Draw a line to match each predator with its prey.

Predator	Prey
1.  •	• deer • polar bear
2.  •	• owl • grasshopper

B. Fill in the blanks. Then for each pair of predator and prey, draw a line to match the characteristic or behavior with each animal.

1. An animal that kills another animal for food is a ______________ .

2. An animal killed by another for food is ______________ .

3. **Predator** and **Prey**

a.

- It has a long tongue.
- It can fly very fast.

b.

- It has powerful jaws.
- It guards while the herd drinks.

c.

- It can see very well.
- It is the same color as the ground.

C. **Look at the classification of animals. Solve the riddles by writing the names of the groups. Then give one more example for each group.**

1. 
I have fur or hair. I feed milk to my young.

_______________ ; e.g. _______________

2. 
I live in water. I have gills for breathing and fins for moving.

_______________ ; e.g. _______________

3. 
My skin is scaly or covered in plates. I lay my eggs on land.

_______________ ; e.g. _______________

4. 
I lay eggs, too, but I have feathers and wings.

_______________ ; e.g. _______________

5. 
I live in water and on land, but I typically lay my eggs in water.

_______________ ; e.g. _______________

D. Read the passage. Then answer the questions.

DINOSAURS

Dinosaurs are extinct. Everything we know about them comes from our study of fossils (the remains or traces of something that lived in prehistoric times). From fossils, we can learn about the way dinosaurs acted and how they looked.

Scientists believe that dinosaurs had no fur, hatched from eggs, and lived on land. Dinosaurs are considered reptiles, though they had features that are quite different from those of reptiles alive today, such as lizards. Lizards move low to the ground and drag themselves around on their bellies, while some dinosaurs walked upright, with their legs directly below their hips.

1. How do scientists learn about dinosaurs?

(A) by studying the fossils of lizards

(B) by studying crocodiles that lived in prehistoric times

(C) by studying the fossils of dinosaurs

2. What are dinosaurs considered to be?

(A) reptiles (B) crocodiles (C) lizards

3. How did a tyrannosaurus rex walk?

(A) like a human, on two legs

(B) like a lizard, dragging itself around on its belly

(C) like a gorilla, on two legs with the help of its two arms

4. What are some characteristics of dinosaurs?

(A) no fur (B) lived in the ocean

(C) had hair (D) lived on land

(E) hatched from eggs

3 Animals – Growth and Changes

All animals change as they grow. In this unit, you will relate young animals to their parents, noting that some look alike and some do not. You will also examine changes in animals as they grow.

After completing this unit, you will

- know what some animals look like at different stages.
- understand that animals can go through many changes.

Vocabulary

reproduce: produce young living things

egg: laid by animals; some have hard shells like chicken eggs and some have soft shells like frog eggs

live young: a baby animal that does not hatch from an egg

Extension

Find pictures of yourself taken at different ages. Place them side by side, starting with the one taken when you were youngest. Take a close look at your facial features in the pictures. Can you see how you have changed as you grew? Ask your parents to show you pictures taken when they were your age. Put their pictures and your pictures side by side to see how much you look like your parents.

A. Number the pictures from 1 to 3 to show the order of growth.

1.

2.

 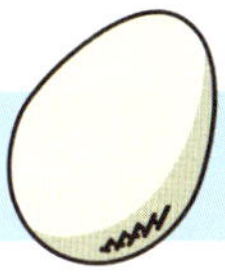 

3.

B. Match the adult animals with their young. Write their names on the lines.

Adult

zebra bear ladybug frog seal

Young

tadpole

foal

cub

pup

nymph

1.  ____________ and ____________

2.  ____________ and ____________

3.  ____________ and ____________

4.  ____________ and ____________

5.  ____________ and ____________

C. Answer the questions. Give examples of animals that are not mentioned in Part B as your answers.

1. Name two animals whose young are called cubs.

____

2. Name one baby animal that looks like its parents.

____

D. Name the animals using the given clues.

mouse   butterfly   duck   frog

1.

I was a caterpillar.

2.

I hatched from an egg in a nest.

3.

I wasn't born as an egg but was a live young.

4.

My tail slowly disappeared as I grew up.

E. Read the passage. Then answer the questions.

Baby Animals

All animals begin their lives as babies. Baby animals might be tiny, but they often have interesting characteristics that they grow out of as they become adults. Growth and changes are amazing parts of an animal's life, and being a baby is an important stage!

Flamingos are well known for their pink bodies, but baby flamingos are born with white feathers. Baby male deer (fawns) are born with white spots and without antlers, but learn to stand very soon after they are born. When pandas are born, they are blind, completely hairless, pink, and tiny – only a little longer than your hand span. When you compare them with a full-grown adult panda, you will see they look nothing like what they will become!

As animals age, they go through magnificent changes. Some baby animals change in predictable ways, but some are completely unrecognizable!

1. Write **T** for true and **F** for false.

   a. All flamingos are pink. ______

   b. Fawns are baby deer. ______

   c. Baby pandas are longer than your arm. ______

   d. All animals change as they grow. ______

2. What is the color of a baby flamingo's feathers?

   (A) pink (B) white (C) brown

3. Which animal is born pink?

   (A) flamingo (B) deer (C) panda

4. Which skill do baby deer learn soon after they are born?

   (A) flying (B) hunting (C) standing

5. Which of the descriptions below describes a baby panda?

   (A) blind, white, tiny

   (B) hairless, tiny, with antlers

   (C) blind, hairless, pink, tiny

4 Life Cycles of Animals

All animals go through life cycles. The stages in a life cycle are similar for all animals, but the growth and changes can be very different. In this unit, you will learn about the different stages of some animals' lives as they go through their life cycles.

After completing this unit, you will

- understand that all animals go through life cycles.
- be able to identify the changes some animals go through in their life cycles.

Vocabulary

life cycle: the series of stages that a living thing goes through in its lifetime

adult: a grown-up

adolescent: an early stage in the process of growing into an adult

Life Cycle of a Butterfly

Extension

Have you seen a caterpillar? Some caterpillars are green, some are colorful, and some are hairy! Being a caterpillar is a stage that some insects go through before they become adults, like butterflies and moths. Most caterpillars feed on leaves – in fact, they eat so much that some people call them "eating machines." They grow very quickly in size, so to adapt to their changing body size, they shed their skin around five times as their bodies grow!

A. Color the Indo-Pacific humpback dolphin to show its skin color at different stages of its life.

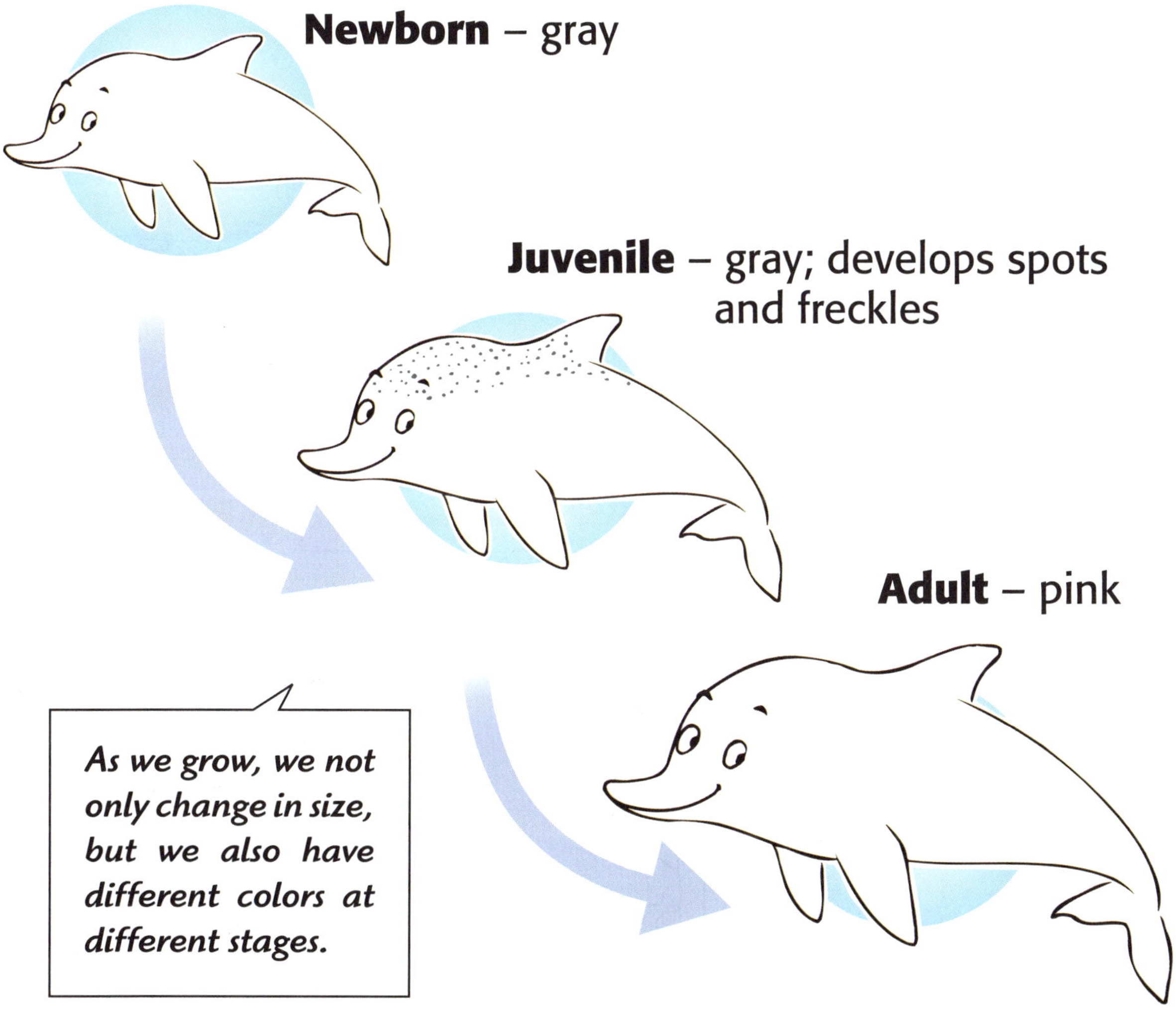

B. The life cycle pictures show what these animals look like as they grow. Write the letters to show the missing stages of life.

1.

2.

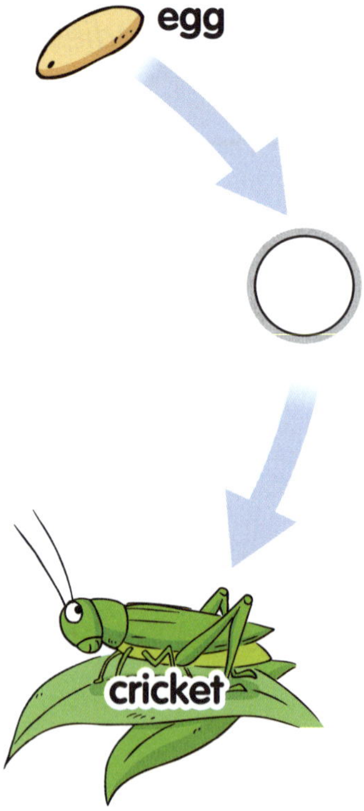

Animals that are born as eggs look very different when they grow up.

3.

C. Read about the life cycle of a monarch butterfly. Then complete the diagram with the words in bold.

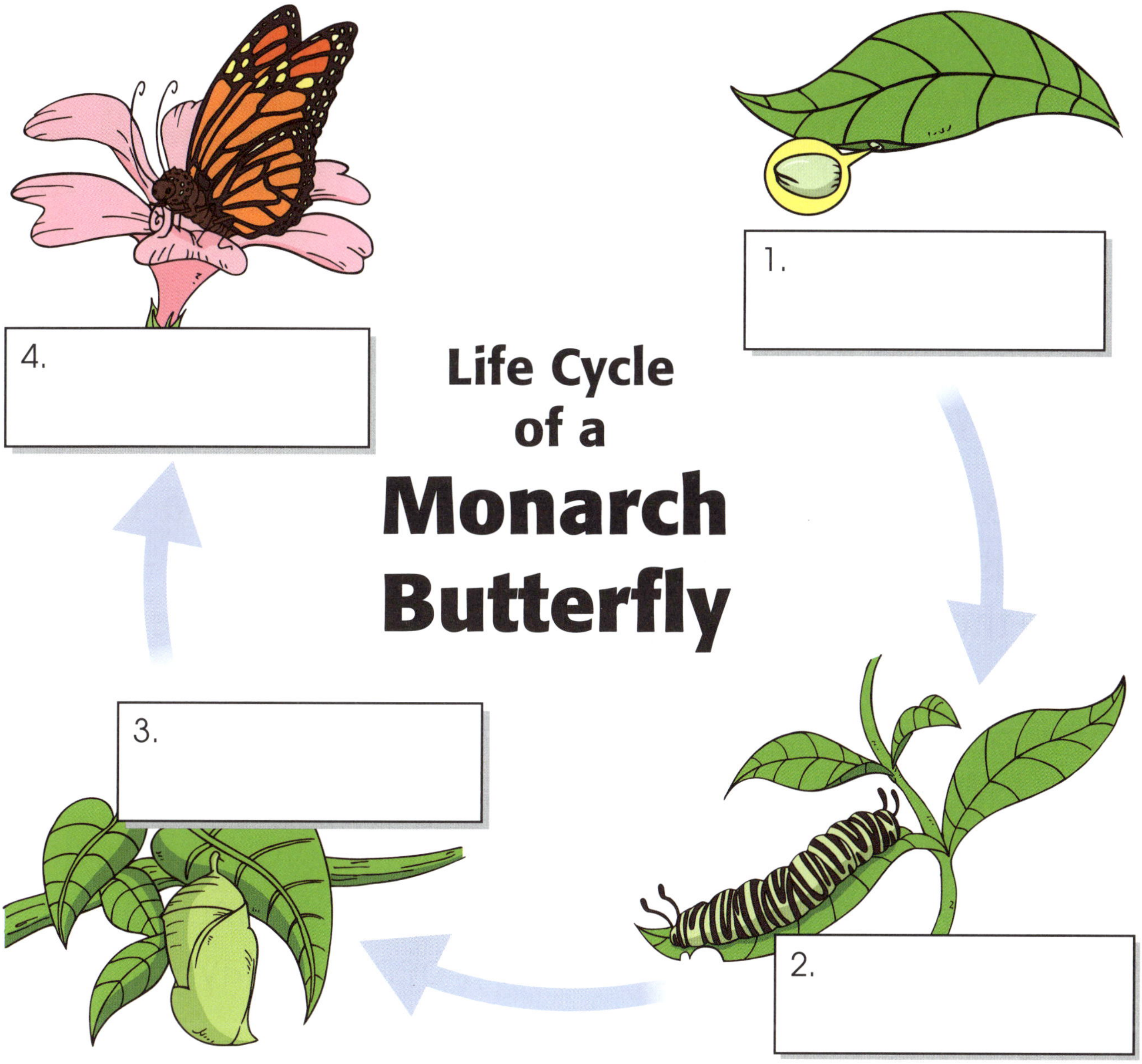

A monarch butterfly lays her **egg** on a leaf. The egg hatches in about five days and becomes a **caterpillar**. The caterpillar then attaches itself to a twig and becomes a **chrysalis**. After about two weeks, a **butterfly** emerges from the chrysalis.

D. Read the passage. Then answer the questions.

The Journey of a Sea Turtle

In the animal kingdom, sea turtles have one of the most incredible life cycles! Although they spend most of their time in water, their lives begin on beaches.

To give birth, the mother sea turtle swims to a beach. She digs a hole in the sand and lays her eggs in it – this is where the life cycle of a baby sea turtle begins. After about 50 days, baby sea turtles, also referred to as hatchlings, break out of their shells and then rush to the water from the beach and begin swimming! They live in water for years and grow, maturing into juvenile (young) turtles, and then into adult turtles. Eventually, they find partners to breed with. They then reach a beach to lay eggs on, and the life cycle continues.

Thanks to this remarkable cycle, sea turtle populations continue to grow over time, and there are always hatchlings ready to rush into the water!

1. Do baby sea turtles hatch from their eggs on land or in water?

____

2. After how many days do sea turtles hatch?

____

3. What do baby sea turtles do after they hatch?

____

____

4. Name two animals that also hatch from eggs.

____

5. Check ✔ where the mother sea turtle lays her eggs.

Ⓐ in the sand

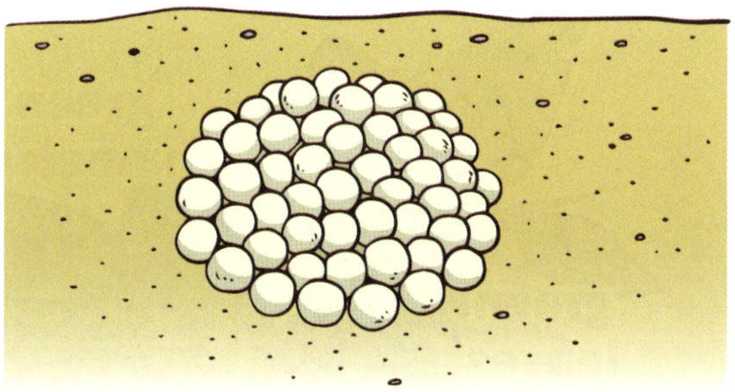

Ⓑ on the sand

5 Animal Adaptations

Animal adaptations describe the ways that help animals live and survive. In this unit, you will learn about the physical and behavioral characteristics that enable animals to survive.

After completing this unit, you will

- learn how an animal's body parts, shape, or covering helps it adapt to its surroundings.
- understand that an animal's behavior plays an important role in its survival.
- know that animal adaptations include camouflage,hibernation, and migration.

Vocabulary

camouflage: the way that animals blend in with their surroundings

hibernation: the method that animals use to sleep through the cold winter

migration: traveling from one place to another

Extension

Camouflage plays an important role in many animals' survival. For example, arctic animals are mostly white to blend into the snow and desert animals are almost all tones of sand-like colors like brownish gray to blend in with the sand. Next time when you go hiking, observe and write down the animals you see. What are their colors? Are their colors similar to the colors of their surroundings?

The brown frog is blending in with the brown bark.

A. Draw lines to match to show how each animal has adapted.

cecropia moth

hedgehog

whale

- Its flippers allow it to steer, turn, and balance.
- It is covered with needlelike spines that can ward off predators.
- Its wings have the pattern of a snake. This is believed to scare predators away.

B. Search online for images of the animals below. Check ✔ to show whether they camouflage through their bodies' colors, patterns, or both.

1\.

My fur turns from brown to white during the winter.

◯ color
◯ pattern

2\.

I'm a master of camouflage.

◯ color
◯ pattern

C. Circle the correct words and the animals that are hibernating.

In winter, food supply runs low and it can be too **cold / hot** for animals to wander about. So some animals find a place and **sleep / run** through the winter to survive. This is called **migration / hibernation** . When an animal hibernates, its body slows down enough to live off of stored fat. As a result, there is **a lot of / little** need for food.

D. Fill in the blanks. Then check ✔ to show which three animals migrate.

winter   place   south

Migrating means traveling from one __________ to another. Canada geese fly __________ every fall to escape the cold __________ and find warm weather and food.

Migrating Animals

- ◯ monarch butterfly
- ◯ cow
- ◯ salmon
- ◯ snake
- ◯ seabird

E. Write whether each animal "camouflages," "hibernates," or "migrates."

1. 

My small wings carry me long distances when needed.

____

2. 

I sleep all winter long.

____

3. 

The bunny can't see me.

____

F. Read the passage. Then answer the questions.

A Mastered Skill: Mimicry

Throughout the natural world, animals do amazing things to survive.

Many use a technique called mimicry, which enables them to take on the appearance of other animals – often ones that are more dangerous or poisonous! While camouflage is about blending into the surroundings, mimicry is about looking like another living thing entirely. This tricks or scares away potential predators and allows the mimicking animal to survive.

At a glance, owl butterflies may not look more special than other butterflies, but these butterflies are masters of mimicry. The big eyelike circles and colors on their wings resemble a scary owl, scaring away predatory birds! Another amazing example is the phylliidae, otherwise known as the "walking leaf." As its name suggests, this insect mimics a leaf, allowing it to move around undetected and fooling predators into thinking that they are just passing by some plants.

1. Write the differences between mimicry and camouflage.

____

____

2. How does mimicry help the mimicking animals survive?

____

____

3. How do the eyespots of owl butterflies help them avoid predators?

   (A) They help the owl butterflies see better.

   (B) They make the owl butterflies look more awake.

   (C) They make the owl butterflies look like owls and scare birds away.

4. How does a "walking leaf" avoid being preyed upon by predators?

   (A) It looks like it is just walking.

   (B) It looks like leaves.

   (C) It grows plant leaves on its body.

6 Human and Animal Interactions

Animals affect us in different ways and human activities have impacts on animals too. Some of these impacts are good, but some are not. In this unit, you will learn about these impacts.

After completing this unit, you will

- understand ways in which animals are helpful to us and ways they can harm us.
- learn how some human activities protect animals and how others harm them.

Vocabulary

interaction: the way two things (e.g. humans and animals) act with each other

national park: an area in which animals and plants are protected from human activities

Extension

Not everyone likes running into a spider, but did you know that most house spiders benefit us? They are predators of common house pests like earwigs, flies, and mosquitoes. By trapping these pests in their spiderwebs, spiders keep these pests from spreading diseases to humans. To know whether you have spiders in your home, walk around and look for spiderwebs! If you can find them, chances are you have spiders in your home!

Thank you for what you do for us.

A. Fill in the blanks to see how animals benefit us in different ways.

How Animals Are Helpful to Us

1. __________ provide us with wool for clothing to keep us warm.

2. __________ can be trained to act as eyes for people who have vision challenges.

3. __________ provide us with honey.

4. __________ provide us with milk.

Interacting with me can calm you down and boost your mood!

B. Fill in the blanks to learn how animals can be harmful to us with the help of the pictures.

How Animals Are Harmful to Us

1. Mosquitoes spread __________ (diseases/pollen) through their bites.

2. Birds destroy __________ (soil/crops) such as apples and blackberries.

3. Bee stings can cause an __________ (allergic/amazing) reaction for some people.

4. Moose on roads can be __________ (dangerous/fun) for drivers.

5. Bears pose a __________ (threat/question) to humans in nature.

C. Read about the human activities that affect animals. Check ✔ the affected animals. Then circle the correct answers.

	Human Activity	Affected Animal	Does it help protect animals?
1.	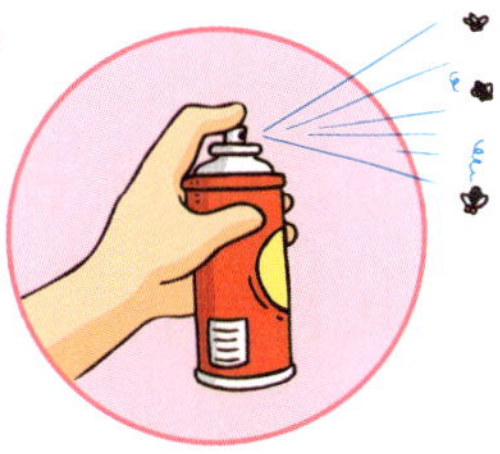 Pesticides are used to kill insects.	◯ mosquito ◯ bear ◯ ant	Yes No
2.	 Animal skin or fur is used to make clothing.	◯ spider ◯ fox ◯ beaver	Yes No
3.	 Unwanted pets are adopted.	◯ giraffe ◯ dog ◯ cat	Yes No
4.	 Land is set aside as protected areas for wildlife reserves.	◯ moose ◯ bear ◯ whale	Yes No
5.	 Wild animals are hunted for leisure.	◯ deer ◯ elephant ◯ sheep	Yes No

D. Read the passage. Then answer the questions.

Dogs – Our Best Friends

You often hear that dogs are our best friends. Have you ever wondered why?

Dogs are great companions for human beings. In fact, this has been the case for thousands of years! Dogs are intelligent, obedient, loyal, and playful, which makes them great service dogs, therapy dogs, and police dogs!

Service dogs are trained to assist owners with disabilities. For instance, they help visually impaired owners move around safely and do their daily tasks. Dogs' loving and playful character also makes them amazing companions to provide therapy for people struggling with emotional issues, giving them comfort and friendship. And because of their intelligence, obedience, and great sense of smell, some dogs are trained to be police dogs, protecting officers and assisting them in finding clues and solving crimes.

1. Write **T** for true and **F** for false.

   a. Dogs are often referred to as our best friends. ____

   b. Therapy dogs help their owners do daily tasks. ____

   c. Police dogs protect and assist officers. ____

2. Write three common character traits of dogs.

   ____

3. Read what the people need. Then draw lines to match them with the dogs that can help them.

to be cheered up •

to do daily tasks •

to help solve crimes •

• 

• 

• 

KEEPING WARM

fat as insulation for animals

Adaptations are particular shapes, forms, and behaviors that animals have developed to help them survive in the particular environment they are in. This is especially important for animals living in very cold or very hot environments because without the right adaptations, it would be very hard for them to survive.

STEM Note

Some fats change form when heated. Like butter, it is solid when it is cold, but when heated, it becomes a liquid.

What you need:

a bucket

fat
(available at dairy stores)

cold water

Difficulty:
●○○○○

Time needed:
15 minutes

In this experiment, you will see how animals living in cold environments use fat to survive.

What to do:

1. Fill the bucket with cold water.
2. Dip your index and middle fingers in one hand into the water. Remember how cold it is.
3. Coat your index and middle fingers in the other hand with fat.
4. Dip your coated fingers into the water.
5. Compare the feelings of the fingers in your hands. Which pair of fingers feels colder?

STEM Note

We often hear that we should eat less high fat foods to stay healthy, but there are good fats that we should eat to keep a balanced diet. Olive oil and fish oil are both examples of good fats.

WHAT *just* happened?

During the experiment, you might have experienced something interesting. The fingers that were coated in fat felt warmer than the fingers that were not coated. Do you know why that happened?

Fat is an excellent insulator, meaning it is good at trapping heat and keeping it from escaping. When you dipped your fingers coated in fat into the cold water, the fat created a protective layer around your fingers like a cozy blanket, preventing the heat from leaving your fingers and keeping them warm.

In nature, animals that live in cold environments, such as polar bears, need lots of fat to stay warm. They have a thick layer of fat under their skin, called blubber, which acts as insulation to keep them warm.

Walruses live in the waters surrounding the Arctic Ocean, where they rely on a thick layer of fat to combat the extreme cold.

STEM INQUIRY

- Do you think the thicker the layer of fat on your fingers, the less cold you will feel from the cold water?
- If your fingers with the fat layer stay in the cold water for a longer period of time, will they feel colder or warmer?

- With the help of an adult, do some research to find out what other adaptations or behaviors animals have to keep warm.

- For many animals living in cold climates, fat acts as an insulating layer to help them keep in body heat. For humans, how do we keep warm in extreme cold? What materials can we use?

- From the experiment, you can see that humans feel temperatures differently due to different factors. Therefore, we need thermometers to measure temperatures. What are the two most commonly used units to measure temperatures?

Fun to know

Fat for Another Use

Fat is not only used for insulation. Some animals store fat for later use as energy. Grizzly bears, for example, purposely eat a lot during summer to get fat. They do this to prepare for winter when there is no food around. Once winter arrives, grizzly bears find a warm place to sleep through the entire winter without eating! They can survive because their body uses the fat they have stored in summer for energy.

EYES ON YOU
how animals' eyes help them survive

In the wild, predators are animals that eat other animals. Those animals that get eaten are called prey. In order to survive, prey have developed special adaptations that help them avoid being eaten.

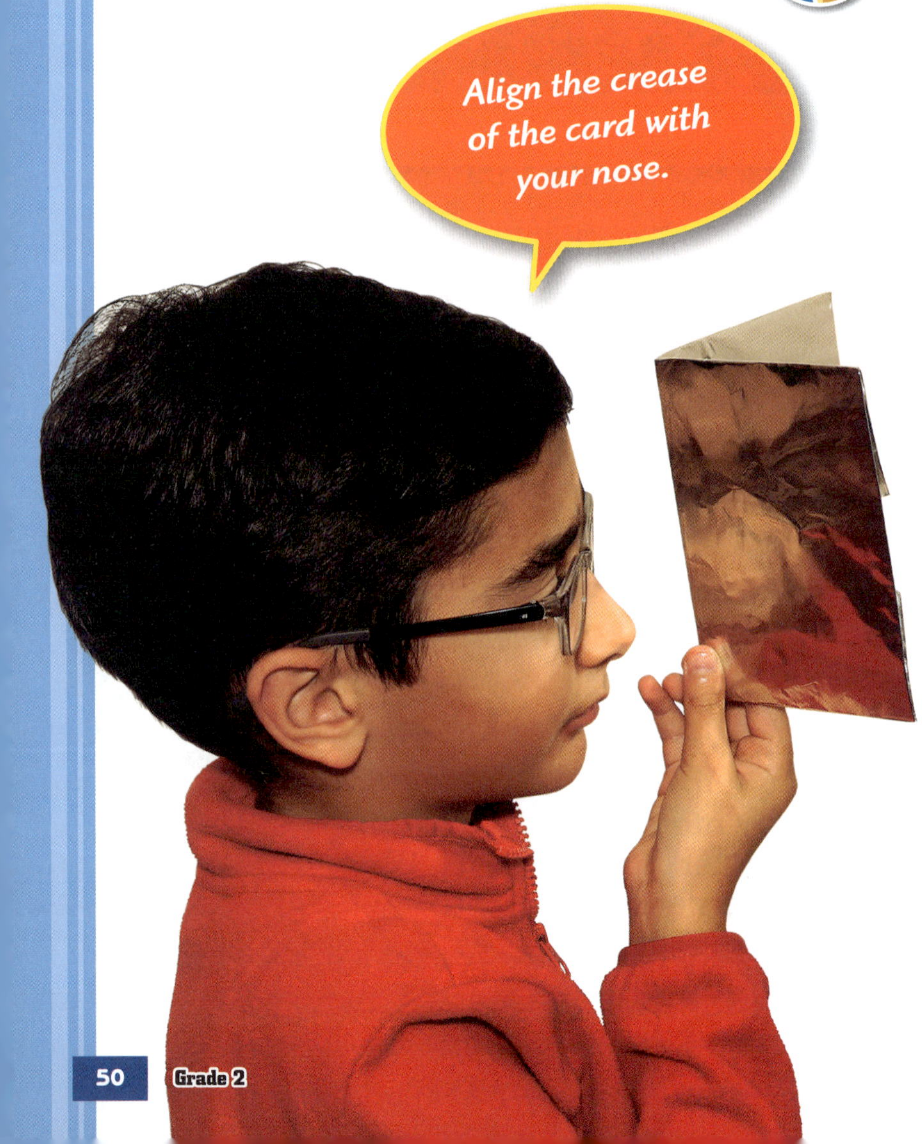

STEM Note

Like a mirror, aluminum foil has a reflective surface, which allows it to reflect images.

Difficulty:
●○○○○

Time needed:
10 minutes

In this experiment, you will learn how some prey use vision to avoid predators.

What you need:

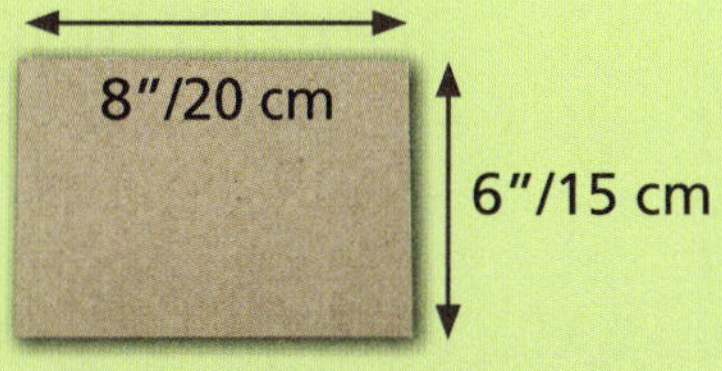

a piece of cardboard from a cereal box

aluminum foil

tape

scissors

What to do:

1. Fold the cardboard in half.
2. Unfold the cardboard. Wrap it with the aluminum foil and secure it with the tape. Try not to wrinkle the foil.
3. Fold the card back and hold it up to your nose.
4. Wave your arm to the side of your head while looking into the card, what do you see?
5. Adjust the card by moving it up and down until you can see movements by the side of your head.

WHAT *just* happened?

The reflection in the card showed you things by the side of your head. In the wild, many prey have eyes located on the sides of their heads, providing a wider field of view, unlike us or other predators whose eyes are in the front. These prey can see more things around them and spot approaching predators without turning their heads.

Imagine a cow with eyes in the front of its head like we do. It would only be able to see what is in front of it. However, with eyes on the sides of its head, it can see predators coming from different directions. This gives the cow a better chance to run away as soon as it feels threatened. Therefore, for prey, having eyes on the sides of their heads is an adaptation that helps them survive in the wild.

- What was the purpose of folding the cardboard in half at the beginning of the experiment?
- How does the lighting condition or background affect the movements observed?

- How will the results be different if the card is wrinkled?
- Can the experiment be done using other materials instead of aluminum foil for similar results? If so, what are those materials?

- An object has symmetry if it can be divided into identical parts. Can you identify symmetries when folding and unfolding the card?
- Is there a specific angle at which the card needs to be folded in order to observe the movements?

Fun to know

Eye Shapes

Did you know that animal eyes are not all the same? Depending on the animals, their eyes have special adaptations to help them survive.

The small black dot in our eyes is called the pupil. In some prey, their pupils stretch horizontally in order to help them see even more of their surroundings. In some predator animals, their pupils stretch vertically, which help them focus on what they are trying to catch.

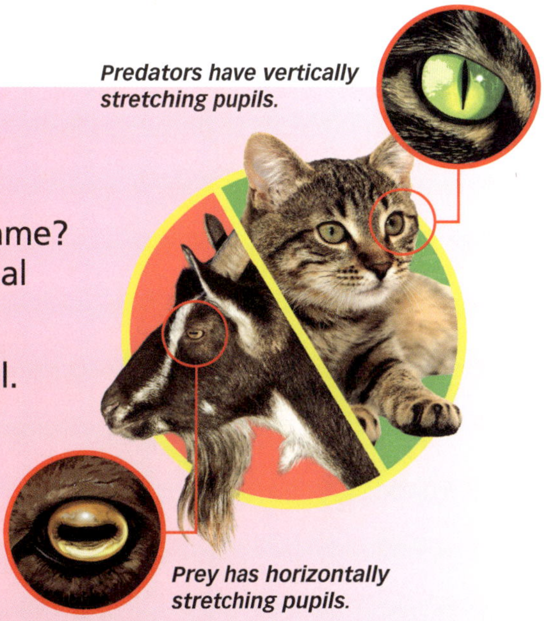
Predators have vertically stretching pupils.

Prey has horizontally stretching pupils.

A FROG'S LIFE

understanding life cycles

Animals go through stages as they grow, but how much change they experience may not be the same. Some animals change a little bit while others, like the frog, change a lot. A frog goes through four different stages in its life cycle: egg, tadpole, froglet, and adult frog. Through the series of changes, frogs adapt to the environment and their bodies transform so that they can survive both in water and on land.

What you need:

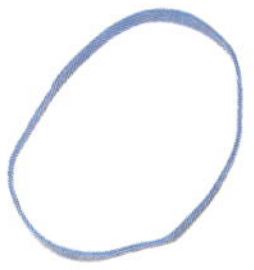

an elastic band

a zipper bag

STEM Note

The "zipper" in zipper bags refers to the plastic tracks that make a strong seal when pressed together. You can open and close them many times, which makes them reusable for different purposes.

Difficulty: ●○○○○

Time needed: 10 minutes

In this experiment, you will learn about the life cycle of a frog and how the changes help frogs adapt to their environment.

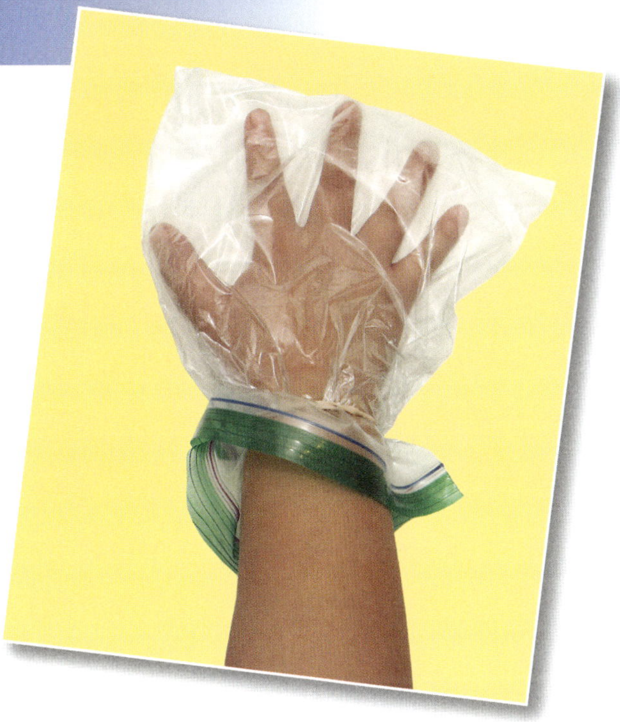

What to do:

1. Fill a sink with water.
2. Put your right hand in the zipper bag. Then tie the elastic band around your wrist to seal the bag.
3. Immerse your left hand in the sink. Spread your fingers and move your hand in the water. Was it easy to move your hand in the water?
4. Immerse your bagged right hand in the sink. Spread your fingers and move your hand in the water. Was it easier or harder to move your hand in the water?

Life Cycle of a Frog

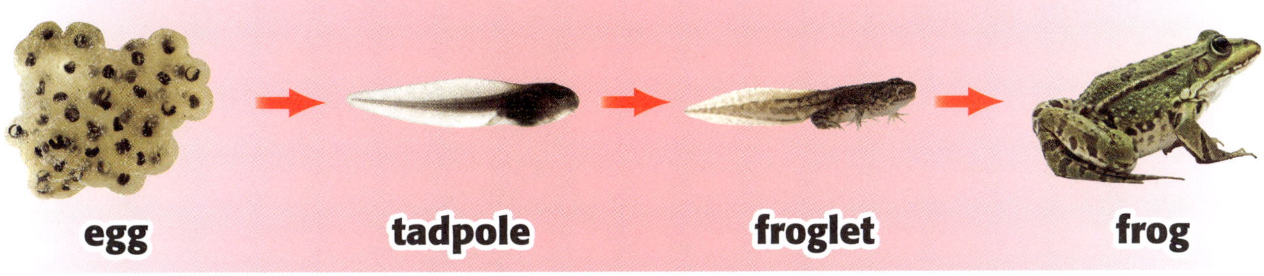

WHAT *just* happened?

a model of frog's foot

You should have noticed that it was harder to move your bagged hand around in the water. This is because your bagged hand had a larger surface area in contact with the water. As a result, you had to use more effort to move your hand. This is similar to the force that a frog exerts to propel itself through water using its webbed feet. Your bagged hand acted like the webbed foot of the frog. A tadpole relies on its long tail to swim freely through the water. However, as it becomes an adult, the frog loses its tail but grows strong legs with webbed feet. These powerful legs and webbed feet make frogs great swimmers and leapers, well adapted to life in water and on land.

Frogs that mainly live on land, in contrast, tend to have shorter legs with no webbed feet. However, they develop other features that help them survive on land, such as round toe pads, which help them walk and climb.

STEM INQUIRY

- What was the purpose of spreading out your fingers in the water for the experiment?
- Webbed feet are a type of adaptation. An adaptation is a physical or behavioral characteristic that an animal or plant has that helps it survive in its environment. What are some other examples of adaptations that aquatic animals have?

- With the help of an adult, research what other animals have webbed feet like frogs. What do these animals have in common?

- In this experiment, you used a zipper bag to simulate a frog's webbed foot. What other materials could you use?
- Frogs use their webbed feet to swim. Design something that can help people swim better.

Fun to know

Beavers

Frogs are not the only animals with webbed feet. Beavers, well-adapted for living near water, have strong webbed feet too. In addition to their feet, beavers have paddle-shaped tails which help them steer through rivers and ponds when moving logs to build their dams.

BUG INSPECTOR
understanding the physical characteristics of insects

Insects are everywhere. You might have bumped into them in your backyard, under rocks, and even in trees. Whether you like it or not, they are the most abundant types of animals in the world. However, not all bugs that you see are insects. So what makes an insect an insect?

What you need:

jars with a lid

a magnifying glass

STEM Note

A magnifying glass makes things appear larger. It helps us examine fine details of things. A typical magnifying glass makes objects look two or three times bigger.

Difficulty:
●●●●●

Time needed:
varies

In this experiment, you will observe and classify insects.

What to do:

1. With an adult, go to your backyard or a park and try to catch some of the bugs listed in the chart on the next page. You may also visit a pet store or museum instead if you cannot find them. Put the bugs in separate jars.
2. Observe each bug using the magnifying glass.
3. Fill out the chart with ✔ or ✘.
4. Release the bugs carefully to their original environment.

My Record

Bug	 Ladybug	 Ant	 Stink Bug	 Grasshopper	 Wood Louse	 Worm
3 Pairs of Legs?						
3 Body Parts?						
1 Pair of Antennae?						

WHAT *just* happened?

The bugs that you observed have different characteristics, such as shape, color, and size. However, for a bug to be an insect, it must have the following:

- 3 pairs of legs
- 1 pair of antennae
- 3 body parts: head, thorax, abdomen

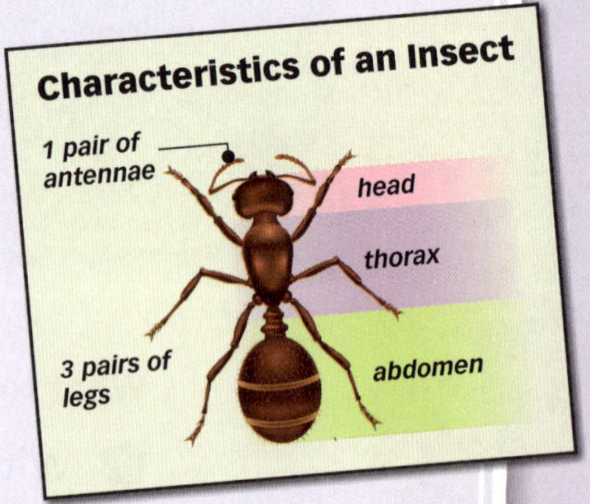

Therefore, the ladybug, ant, stink bug, and grasshopper are all insects while the other bugs are not. When you observed the insects closely, were you able to see their antennae move around? This is because insects use their antennae to smell, taste, and sense the world around them. Some insects also use their antennae to communicate.

STEM INQUIRY

- Not all of the bugs we see are insects. Try to collect a bug that is not an insect. Draw a picture of the bug you collected. Label the body parts that are similar to the parts of an insect.

- With the help of an adult, research the insects that are native to your area. How many of the native insects are you able to find in your local area?

- Use materials you can find around your home to create a 3D insect model.

- What is the best unit of measurement to measure the insects you collected? Make a list of the insects in order from smallest to largest.

Fun to know

Bug Built Kingdoms

Some insects enjoy living alone while some, such as bees and ants, live in communities called colonies. Individuals in a colony work together as a team to take care of one another and to keep the colony going. Within each colony, there is a queen. The rest of the members are either soldiers, who protect the nest, or workers, who look for food, build the nest, and keep things running in general.

a beehive

the opening of an anthill

Section 2

Structures and Mechanisms

1 Position

Position describes the location of an object. There are stationary and moving objects. In this unit, you will describe the positions of objects and understand that their positions change when they are moving.

After completing this unit, you will

- know about positions of objects in relation to other objects.
- be able to identify stationary and moving objects.
- know how the position of an object can be changed.

Vocabulary

position: the location of an object

clockwise: the direction of a clock hand's movement

counterclockwise: the opposite of clockwise

Extension

"Near" and "far" are words that describe one position in comparison to another. Some things can be described as both "near" and "far."

*My grandma's house is **near** enough to drive to but too **far** to walk to.*

*The plane was **near** enough to be seen but too **far** away to be heard.*

A faraway object may be described as being near compared to something farther away.

*The park is **near** my home compared to the store.*

Can you think of something that is both near and far? How about something far which is near compared to something else?

A. Identify the stationary and moving objects. Write the letters. Then circle the correct answer.

1. Stationary Objects: ____________

   Moving Objects: ____________

2. Dave is standing **far from / near** the finish line.

B. Look at the picture. Describe where the things are using the given position words.

above in in front of beside under on behind

1. The toy fish is ____________ the cat.

2. The girl is ____________ the chair.

3. The basket is ____________ the chair.

4. The cat is ____________ the chair.

5. The shovel is ____________ the pail.

6. The girl is ____________ the toy mouse.

7. The ball of yarn is ____________ the cat.

C. Look at the objects. Write "stationary" or "moving" in the boxes. Then complete the sentences.

1.

2. Julia is going to put a toy car and a mug on a balance. If the toy car is heavier than the mug, the toy car will go ____________ and the mug will go ____________ .
up/down (under each blank)

D. Read the passage. Then answer the questions.

GPS: Global Positioning System

"You have arrived at your destination" – this is what you might have heard from your parent's phone or car on a road trip. The GPS, or Global Positioning System, is a system that can locate our exact position on Earth. This satellite-based navigation system is made up of three parts: satellites, receivers, and ground stations.

- satellite:
  an object that revolves around Earth in space
- receiver:
  a device that receives signals from more than one satellite and calculates your exact location
- ground station:
  a hub that communicates with satellites by sending and receiving signals

The GPS is a great invention that helps us travel anywhere at any time in the world.

1. What does GPS stand for?

(A) Ground Positioning Station
(B) Global Positioning System
(C) Global Positioning Satellites

2. What is the GPS made up of?

(A) satellites, receivers, ground stations
(B) phones, ground stations, signals
(C) satellites, signals, phones

3. Label the major parts of the GPS. Then draw lines to show the receiving signals from the satellites to the receiver.

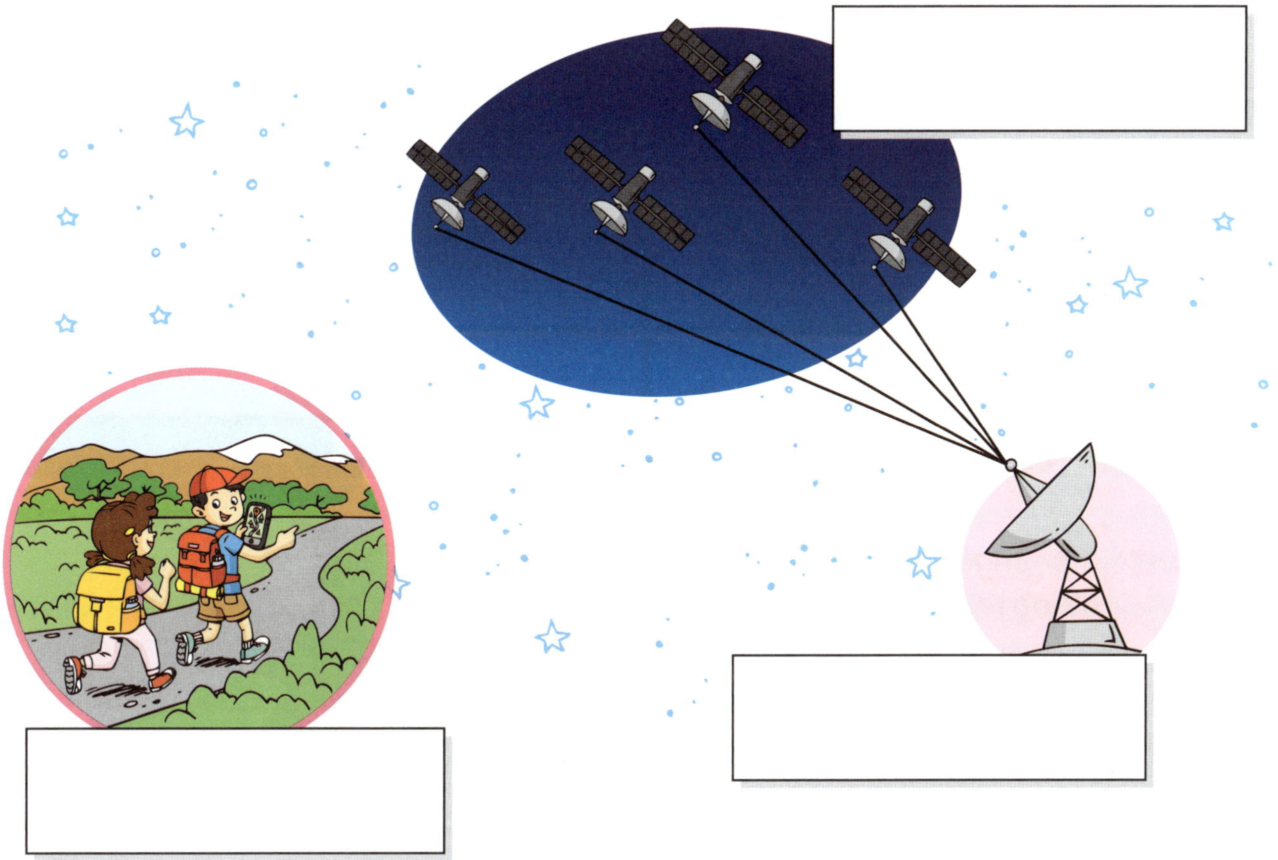

2 Movement

When something is pulled or pushed, it often moves. In this unit, you will learn that a push or a pull can cause movement and describe the movement it causes.

After completing this unit, you will

- understand different ways in which objects move.
- know that movements can change the position of an object.

Vocabulary

movement: a change in position of an object

vibrate: to tremble or shake

Extension

Kayaking is a fun water activity. But did you know that kayaking involves both pushing and pulling the paddle for every stroke? To go forward, slice one blade into the water and pull it toward you while pushing the other blade away from you. On the next stroke, slice the other blade into the water and pull while pushing the other end. Keep repeating these movements to kayak and have fun!

A. Write "push" or "pull" to describe each action which causes movement.

1. __________ a baby stroller.
2. __________ a wagon.
3. __________ the buttons on a keyboard.
4. __________ the door away from you to open it.
5. __________ the string to turn on the light.

B. Write how you would complete each part of the obstacle course.

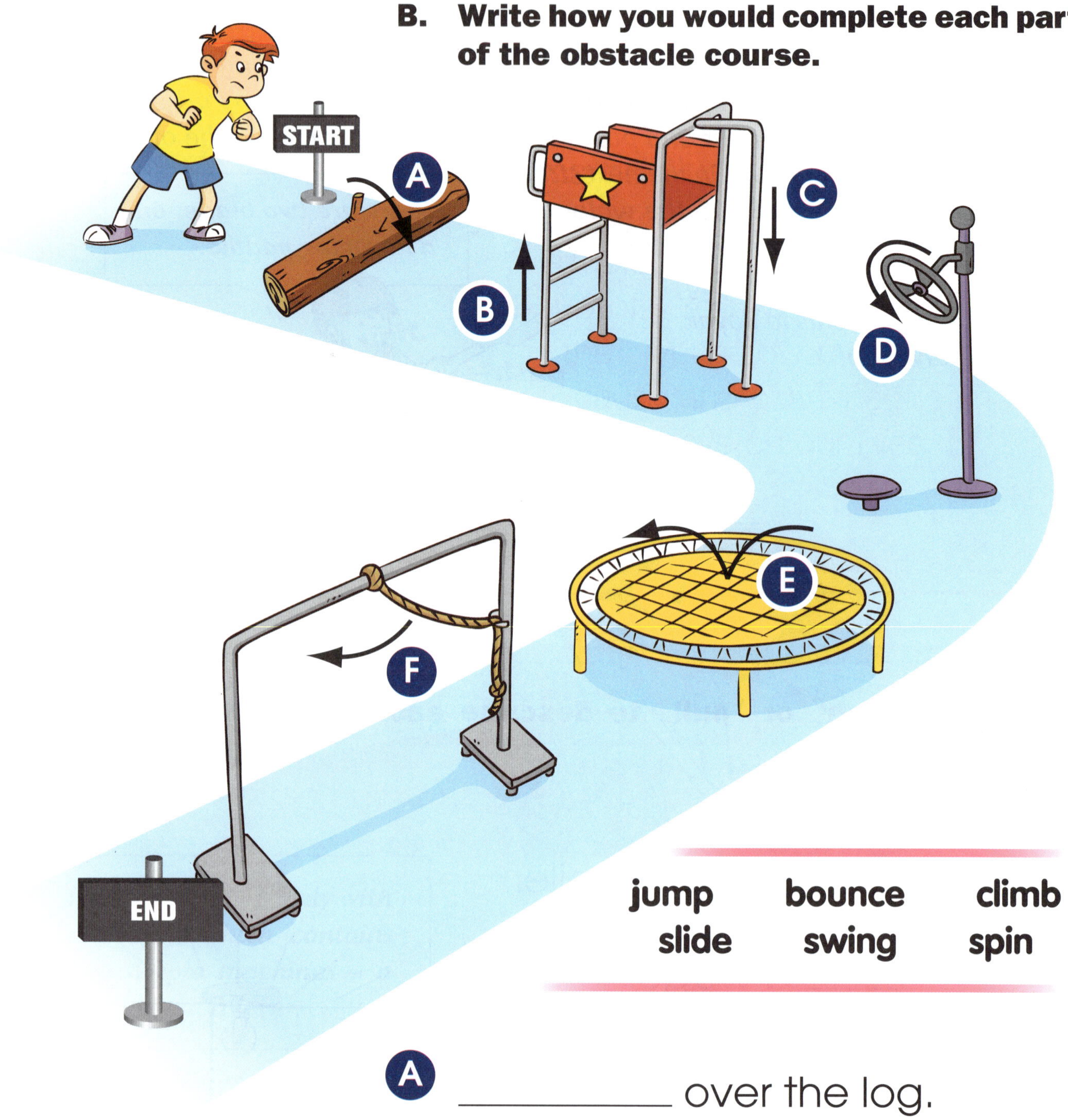

jump	bounce	climb
slide	swing	spin

A ____________ over the log.

B ____________ up the ladder.

C ____________ down the pole.

D ____________ the wheel.

E ____________ off the trampoline.

F ____________ on the rope.

C. Write the correct words to describe the movements.

swinging bouncing rolling vibrating spinning sliding turning

1.

____

2.

____

3.

____

4.

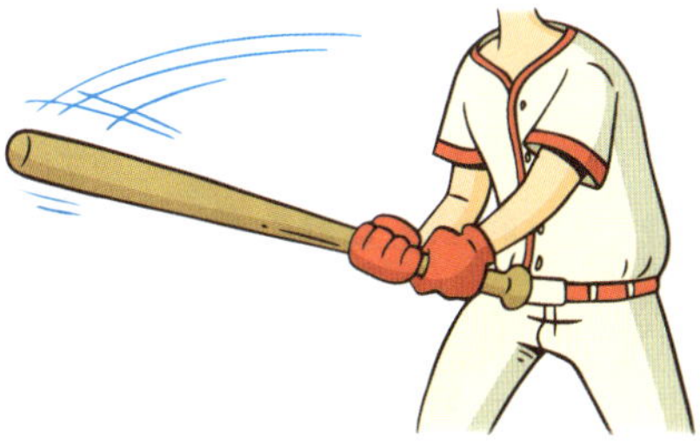

____

5.

____

6.

____

7.

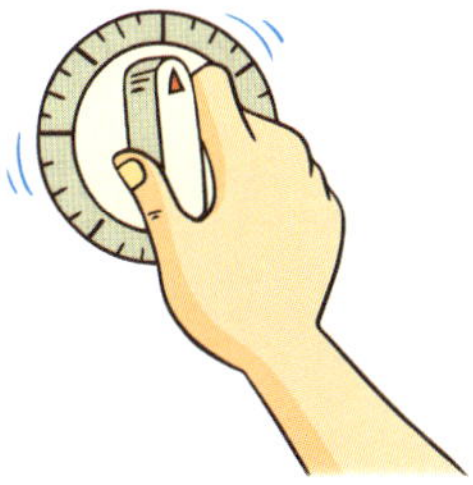

____

D. Read the passage. Then answer the questions.

Toys in Motion

Toy cars can show you the ways you can make objects move. You can pull a toy car toward you or push it away from you; the stronger you push or pull, the farther it will travel.

Another great toy in motion is the basketball. You can bounce it, spin it on your finger, or roll it across the floor.

Having fun with a jump rope also involves a lot of movements. You spin the rope to get it over your head and under your feet, and you jump over it to keep it in motion.

Toys are probably something you know a lot about, and they can help you understand many things about motion.

1. Describe how strong the push was for each toy car. Write the letters.

A **light push** **B** **strong push** **C** **very strong push**

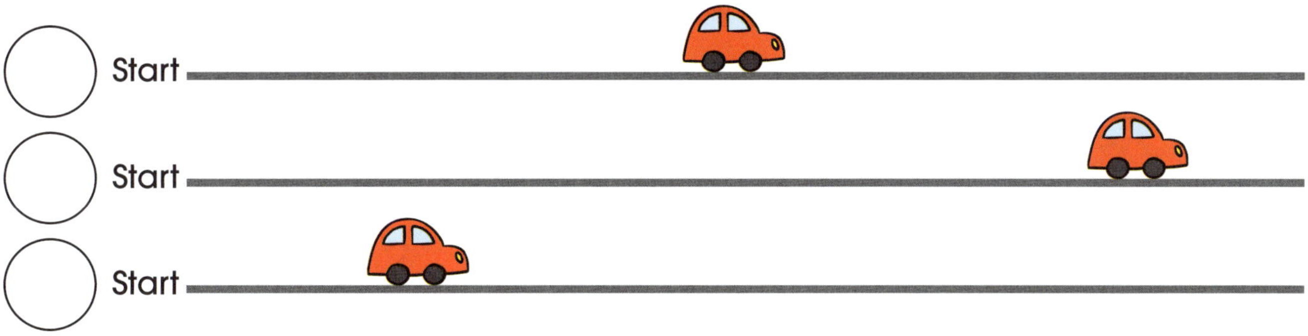

2. In what ways can you move a basketball?

____

____

3. What movements are involved when you use a jump rope?

____

____

4. Draw a toy that moves and describe its movements.

____

____

____

3 Simple Machines (1)

There are six basic types of simple machines. In this unit, you will explore three of them: a lever, an inclined plane, and a wedge. You will see how they make objects move and how they make work easier.

After completing this unit, you will

- know what a lever, an inclined plane, and a wedge are.
- understand that using simple machines is part of our daily lives.
- understand that simple machines make our lives easier.

It is much easier to open this can with a pry, which is a lever – a type of simple machine.

Vocabulary

simple machine: a device that makes work easier

work: the force needed to move an object

load: something to be carried

Extension

We often think of simple machines as something made by us, but they are found in nature, too!

Think of an alligator's jaws closing on its prey. They work exactly like a tool we use for cracking nuts – the nutcracker! Both the alligator's jaws and the nutcracker are levers.

Compare other things in nature to simple machines. You will find that there are many simple machines around us.

A. Identify and name each simple machine. Then match it with the correct description. Write the letter in the circle.

wedge   inclined plane   lever

______

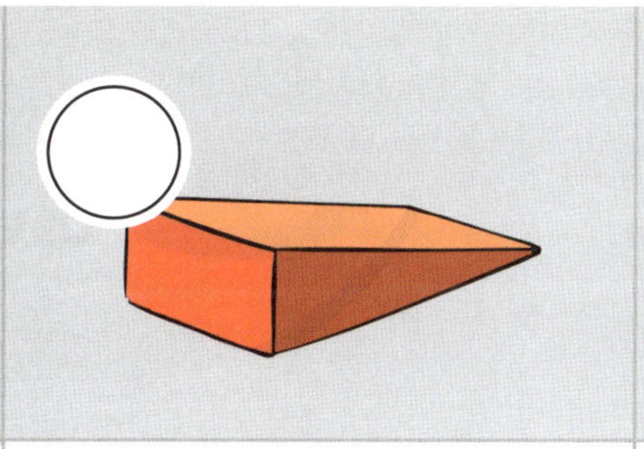

______

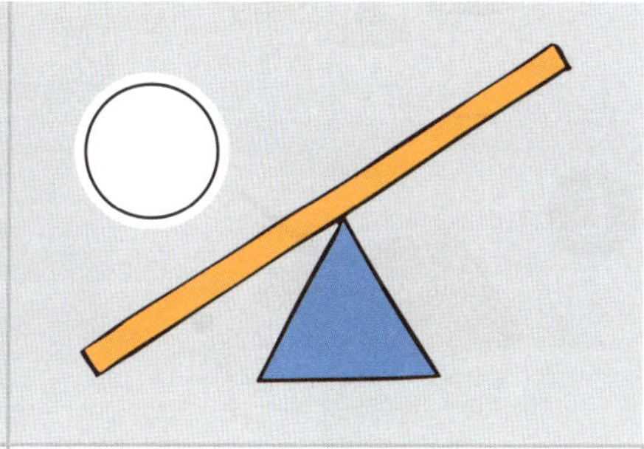

______

(A) a slanted edge that pushes something apart

(B) a sloped surface that helps move a load up or down

(C) a stick or board that uses a resting point to move a load

B. Draw a line to match each tool with its purpose. Then identify the type of simple machine each tool is.

A

B

C
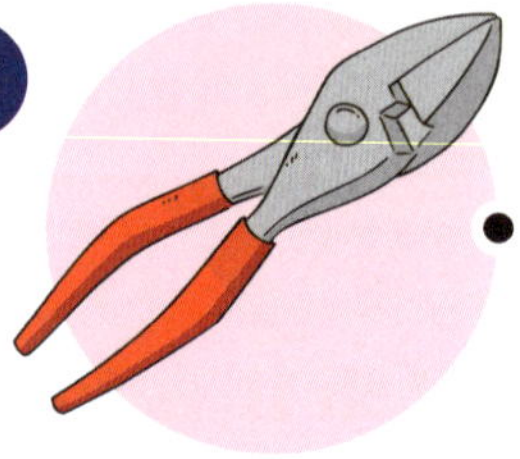

D

E

F
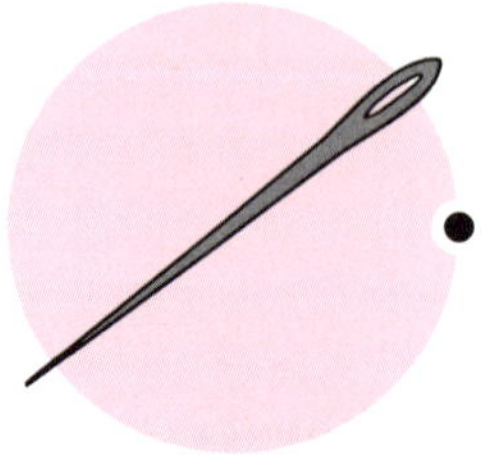

- to lift a piano onto the back of a truck
- to pry a piece of wood into smaller pieces
- to hold wires and bend them
- to allow water to run off
- to pierce a piece of fabric
- to compare objects' weights

Lever:

______ , ______

Inclined Plane:

______ , ______

Wedge:

______ , ______

C. **Name the simple machine shown in each picture. Then give one more example of that type of simple machine.**

A

B

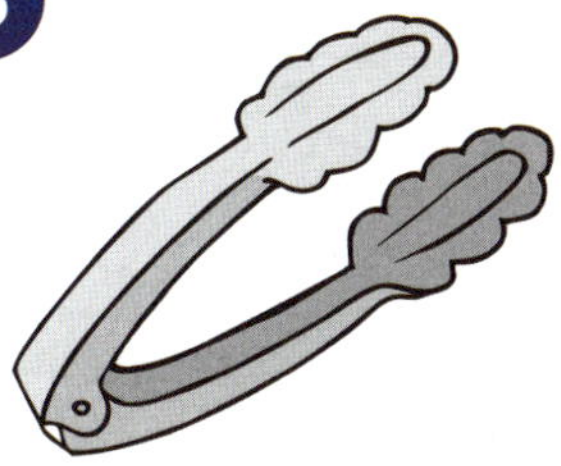

C

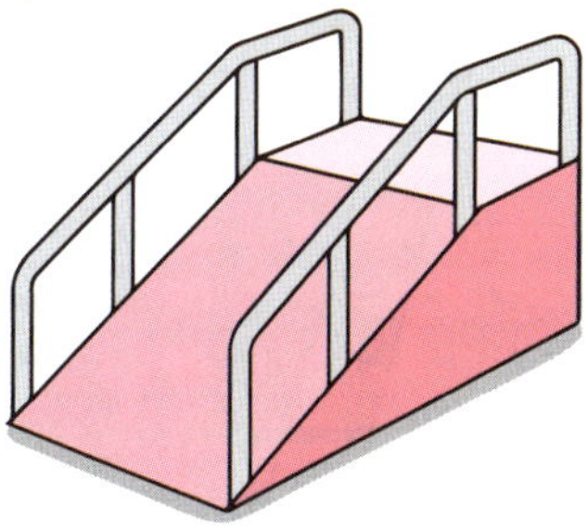

D

E

F

A ____________________

e.g. ____________________

B ____________________

e.g. ____________________

C ____________________

e.g. ____________________

D ____________________

e.g. ____________________

E ____________________

e.g. ____________________

F ____________________

e.g. ____________________

D. Read the passage. Then answer the questions.

Inclined Planes:
Simple, Useful Machines

Inclined planes are simple machines. They make moving objects up easier than if they were lifted, and they help us move them down with more care than if they were dropped.

Slides are great examples. They give you the thrill of falling but get you safely to the ground. Ski hills are examples of inclined planes in nature. Useful inclined planes include those built to load trucks with cargo and those built for people who use wheelchairs so that they can access buildings. These inclined planes are called ramps.

Imagine you are building a ramp for people who need one to access a restaurant. Would you build a short, steep ramp from the ground to the door, or a long ramp that is not steep?

1. Check ✔ the examples of an inclined plane.

2. Give an example of an inclined plane used in parks and an example of one found in nature.

3. What helps people access buildings without using stairs? What type of simple machine is it?

4. Color the inclined plane that makes it easier and safer to move up and down.

4 Simple Machines (2)

In the previous unit, you learned about three types of simple machines. In this unit, you will be introduced to the remaining three types – a pulley, a wheel and axle, and a screw. You will also explore how they make work easier.

After completing this unit, you will

- know what a pulley, a wheel and axle, and a screw are.
- understand that simple machines make our daily lives easier.

Vocabulary

axle: a rod that passes through the middle of a wheel

auger: a drilling device

Extension

Fastening objects is one of the most common functions of screws. However, as a simple machine, a screw has other practical uses, too. Ice fishing is an enjoyable activity during cold winters. To make a hole in the ice for fishing, a hand auger (a modified version of a screw) is used. Using a hand auger is easy – just twist and turn and a hole is drilled!

A. Name each simple machine. Then draw lines to match.

pulley   wheel and axle   screw

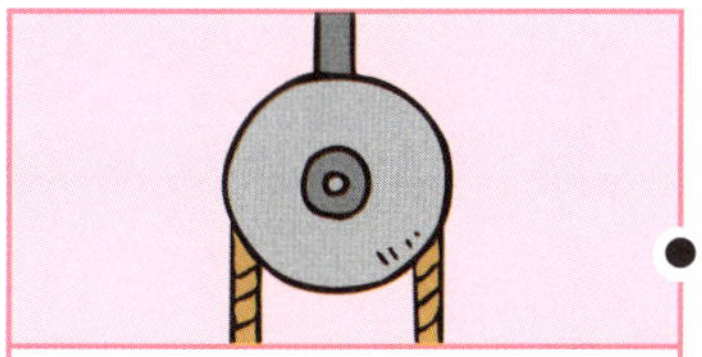

- a wheel with a groove and a rope that moves along that groove
- an inclined plane wrapped around a rod
- a rod in the middle of a wheel that is able to rotate

B. Draw a line to match each machine with its function. Then identify what type of simple machine it is. Write the letter.

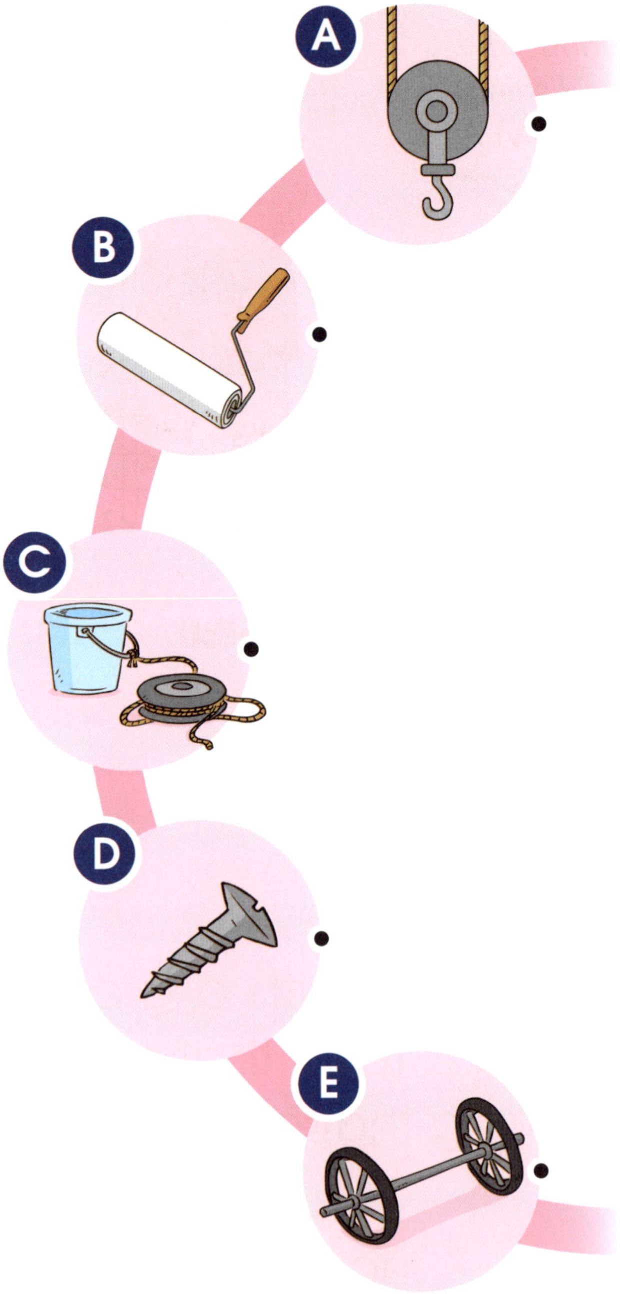

Function

- to roll paint onto surfaces
- to attach a coat hook to the wall
- to move things as part of a crane
- to get water from a well
- to move things as part of a cart

Pulley	Wheel and Axle	Screw

C. Name the simple machine shown in each picture. Then give one more example of that type of simple machine.

1.

e.g. ____________________

2.

e.g. ____________________

3.

e.g. ____________________

4.

e.g. ____________________

5.

e.g. ____________________

6.

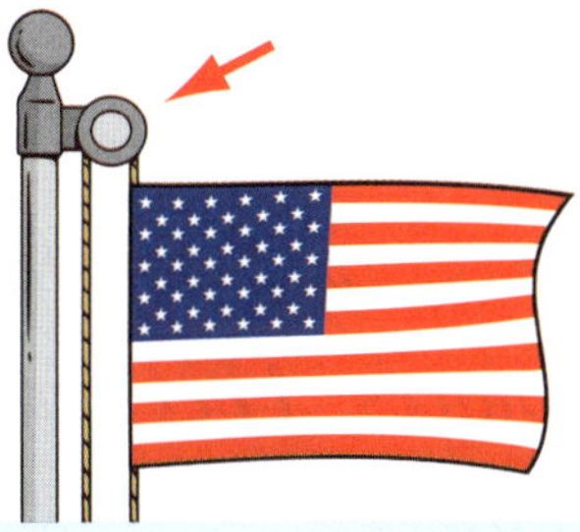

e.g. ____________________

D. Read the passage. Then answer the questions.

Simple Machines Everywhere

Dear Diary,

I had so much fun playing a scavenger hunt with my class today.

My teacher Mrs. White came up with the idea. My class was asked to hunt for simple machines, such as a wheel and axle, screw, and pulley. It surprised me that we could find them all at school!

In our classroom, it took me no time to spot the wheels and axles in Mrs. White's swivel chair. The wheels allow Mrs. White to move easily when she is on the chair. For the screw, it surprised me that screws not only were used to fasten the bulletin board to the wall but were also used in my water bottle. The rim of the bottle and the inside of its cap are both screws that keep the water from spilling.

Guess who found a pulley in the schoolyard. It was me! I found it attached up high on the flagpole. With the help of the pulley, we can easily set the flag high up on the pole.

Mrs. White said simple machines can be found in many places. I bet I can find a lot at home!

Stacy

1. Circle the simple machine in each picture. Then name it.

____

____

____

____

2. Draw a line to match each object with the simple machine it uses. Then give an example of each type of simple machine from your own home.

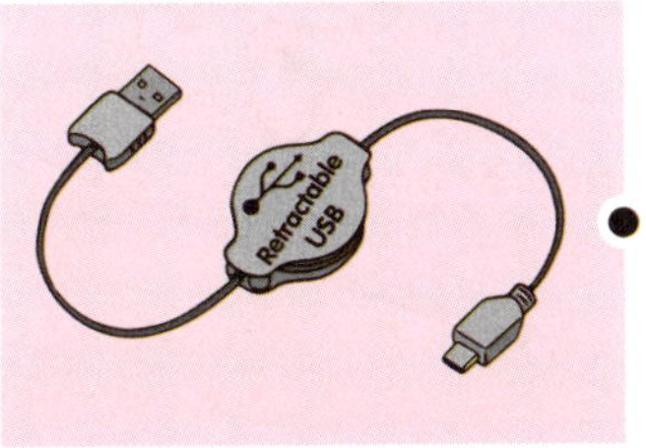

- **Screw:**

____
example

- **Pulley:**

____
example

- **Wheel and Axle:**

____
example

5 Machines in Action

Mechanisms help us move things. In this unit, you will look at mechanisms and the simple machines they are made up of. You will learn to describe the types of movement they cause and examine the impacts they have on our lives.

After completing this unit, you will

- understand that mechanisms are made up of two or more simple machines.
- know that mechanisms change the type or direction of movement.
- understand how mechanisms are useful to us.

I can dig a hole easily with a shovel, which contains two simple machines – a wedge and a lever.

Vocabulary

mechanism: a device made up of two or more simple machines

friction: a force that resists movement

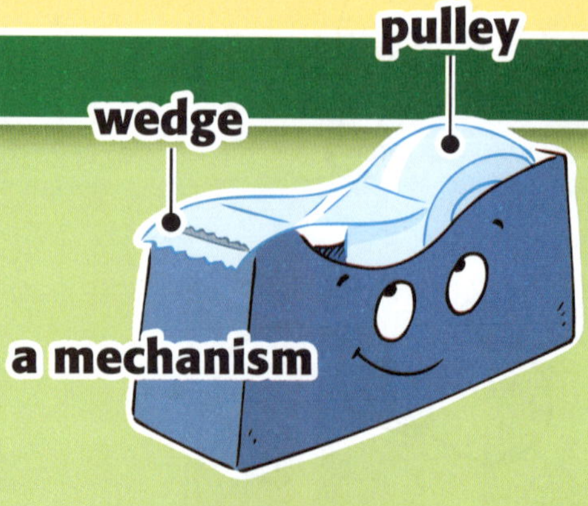

Extension

Wherever there is movement, there is friction. Friction resists movement. Sometimes that is good. When we walk, we need enough friction between our shoes and the ground so that we do not slip. When we skate on ice, we want less friction so we can move fast and freely.

> *A little or a lot, friction goes hand in hand with mechanisms. Think of the friction needed for the different uses of an inclined plane.*

More Friction
e.g.
- parking garage ramp
- pedestrian ramp down to a dock

Less Friction
e.g.
- waterslide
- bobsled track

A. Which simple machines are the mechanisms made up of? Complete the names of the simple machines.

1.

handles

- l__ __e__

blades

- __e__g__

2.

handles

- __e__ __r

wheel

- wh__ __l and __ __le

B. Draw lines to match the movements with the mechanisms.

Movements

Movements	Mechanisms
round and round •	• eggbeater
up and down •	• door hinge
back and forth •	• elevator
straight •	• bike pedals
	• sliding doors
	• printer

C. Name a mechanism that has each movement.

Round and Round

Up and Down

Back and Forth

Straight

D. Match the mechanisms with the correct situations based on the purposes they serve. Write the letters. Then give another example of a mechanism for each situation.

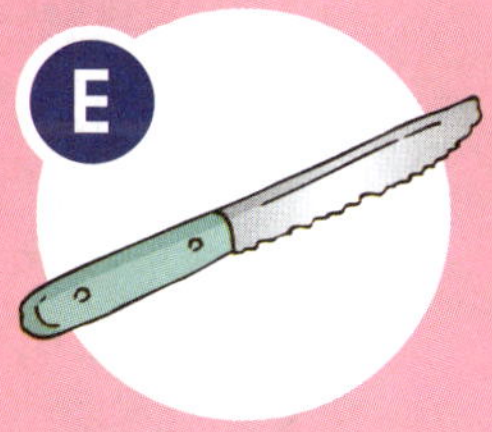

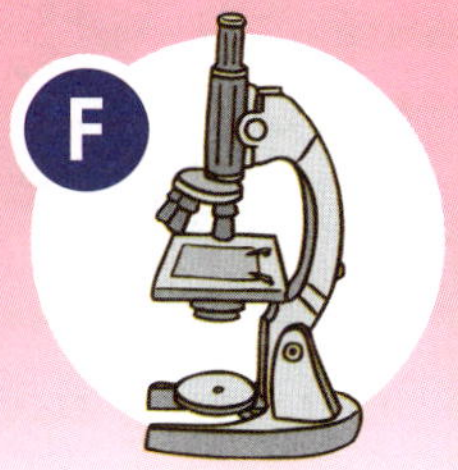

1.  cooking

   e.g. ____ ; ______________

2.  construction

   e.g. ____ ; ______________

3.  farming

   e.g. ____ ; ______________

4.  recreation

   e.g. ____ ; ______________

5.  science

   e.g. ____ ; ______________

6.  transportation

   e.g. ____ ; ______________

E. Read the passage. Then answer the questions.

The Thrill of Movement in Amusement Parks

There are many types of thrilling rides in amusement parks, but most move in very similar ways: back and forth, round and round, and up and down.

The **pirate ship** moves back and forth, making you feel like you are swinging. The **teacups** feature large teacup-shaped carts spinning round and round while the floor beneath them spins round and round too! The **Ferris wheel** spins round and round and its riders move up and down in a circular motion. Can you guess what the **carousel**'s two movements are as you sit on one of its beautifully painted horses, holding a golden pole? Its floor moves round and round, but your horse moves up and down, as if it were galloping.

1. Trace the dotted lines. Then describe the movements of the thrilling rides.

Pirate Ship

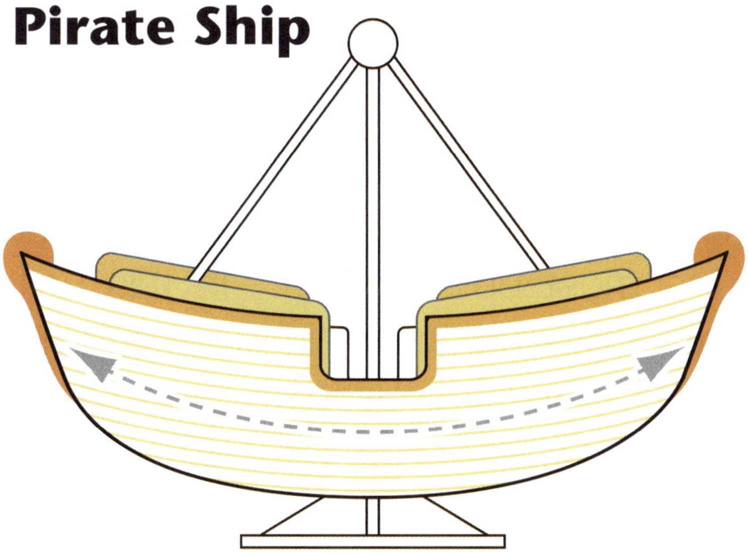

Movement:

____

Teacups

Movement:

____

2. Which two movements are involved in a carousel? Name the part that shows each movement.

____

____

6 Uses of Simple Machines

Knowing the uses of different simple machines is important because it allows us to get the most out of them. In this unit, you will learn how simple machines should be used to help us do work. You will also learn to use simple machines safely.

After completing this unit, you will

- know the uses of simple machines.
- know how to modify a simple machine to make it even better.

Vocabulary

emissions: harmful gases from machines that pollute the air

goggles: protective eyewear

Extension

Machines make our lives easier in many ways by allowing us to do things more efficiently and with less effort. However, they also have their drawbacks. Many heavy-duty machines, like excavators and bulldozers, are powered by gas and diesel. These machines are robust, but their emissions pollute the air. And because of how powerful these machines are, the flying dust that results from heavy drilling, grinding, and sawing pollutes the air. It is difficult to completely avoid the harm to the environment caused by machines, but there are things we can do to help. For example, instead of driving, we can walk or bike whenever possible.

A. Fill in the blanks to complete the descriptions of the uses of the simple machines.

1. 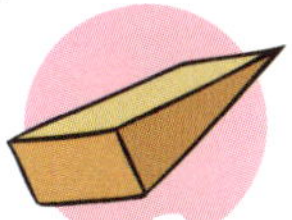
wedge
separates something by ____________ (pulling/cutting), piercing, or splitting

2. 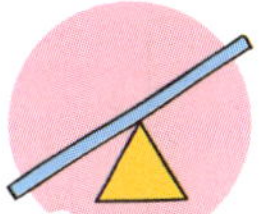
lever
____________ (holds/raises) or moves a load

3. 
wheel and axle
turns or ____________ (raises/moves) objects

4. 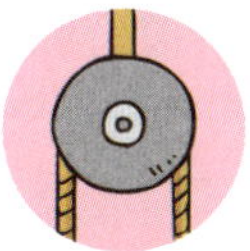
pulley
moves objects up, ____________ (down/left), and across long distances

5. 
screw
raises and lowers things and ____________ (moves/holds) things together

6. 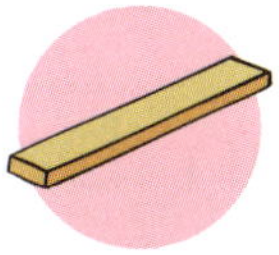
inclined plane
makes the work of moving objects ____________ (up and down/away) easier

B. Name the simple machine that is used in each picture. Then check ✔ the correct picture to show which simple machine makes work easier and fill in the blanks.

1.

Simple Machine:

____

The Better One:

With a ______________________ (longer/shorter) plane, objects can be moved with less effort.

2.

Simple Machine:

____

The Better One:

With a ______________________ (sharper/blunter) edge, objects can be cut with less effort.

C. **Circle the correct words for the rules.**

Rules to Follow When Working with Machines

- ✔ Carry and use scissors and other cutting tools **carelessly / safely** .
- ✔ Keep the work space **clean / dirty** and tidy.
- ✔ Return tools, materials, and equipment where they belong **before / after** using them.
- ✔ **Untie / Tie up** long hair while working.
- ✔ **Remove / Wear** jewelry before working, including rings, necklaces, and bracelets.
- ✔ When needed, wear goggles to protect the **eyes / mouth** .

D. Read the passage. Then answer the questions.

The Most Famous "Machine"

by **Rube Goldberg**

Rube Goldberg was a famous American engineer and cartoonist. He is known for creating "Rube Goldberg machines" – inventions that did simple jobs in complicated ways. One of the most famous of these is the Self-Operating Napkin, a machine with a multistep process involving birds and rockets just to wipe a man's chin.

Even though it looks complicated, this silly invention is made up of a series of simple machines! Raising the spoon pulls the string, which moves the ladle and knocks the cracker into the air. The parrot jumps to catch the cracker, shaking the perch and knocking the seeds into the pail below. (Are you still with me?) As the pail is now heavier, it pulls the string, which opens the lighter and ignites the rocket. When the rocket flies off, it causes the sickle to cut the string, freeing the napkin to swing back and forth on the man's chin. When taken together, it is hilariously complex. But at the heart of this machine are just some simple movements: pushing, pulling, lifting, and cutting.

Self-Operating Napkin

1. Who is Rube Goldberg?

____

2. What are Rube Goldberg machines?

____

____

3. Put the steps of the Self-Operating Napkin's process in order from 1 to 7.

(1) The man raises the spoon which pulls the string and moves the ladle.

◯ The lighter ignites the rocket.

◯ The ladle knocks the cracker into the air.

◯ The pail, weighted down with the seeds, pulls the string and opens the lighter.

◯ The napkin is freed to swing back and forth on the man's chin.

◯ The rocket flies off, causing the sickle to cut the string.

◯ The parrot jumps to catch the cracker, shaking the perch and knocking the seeds into the pail.

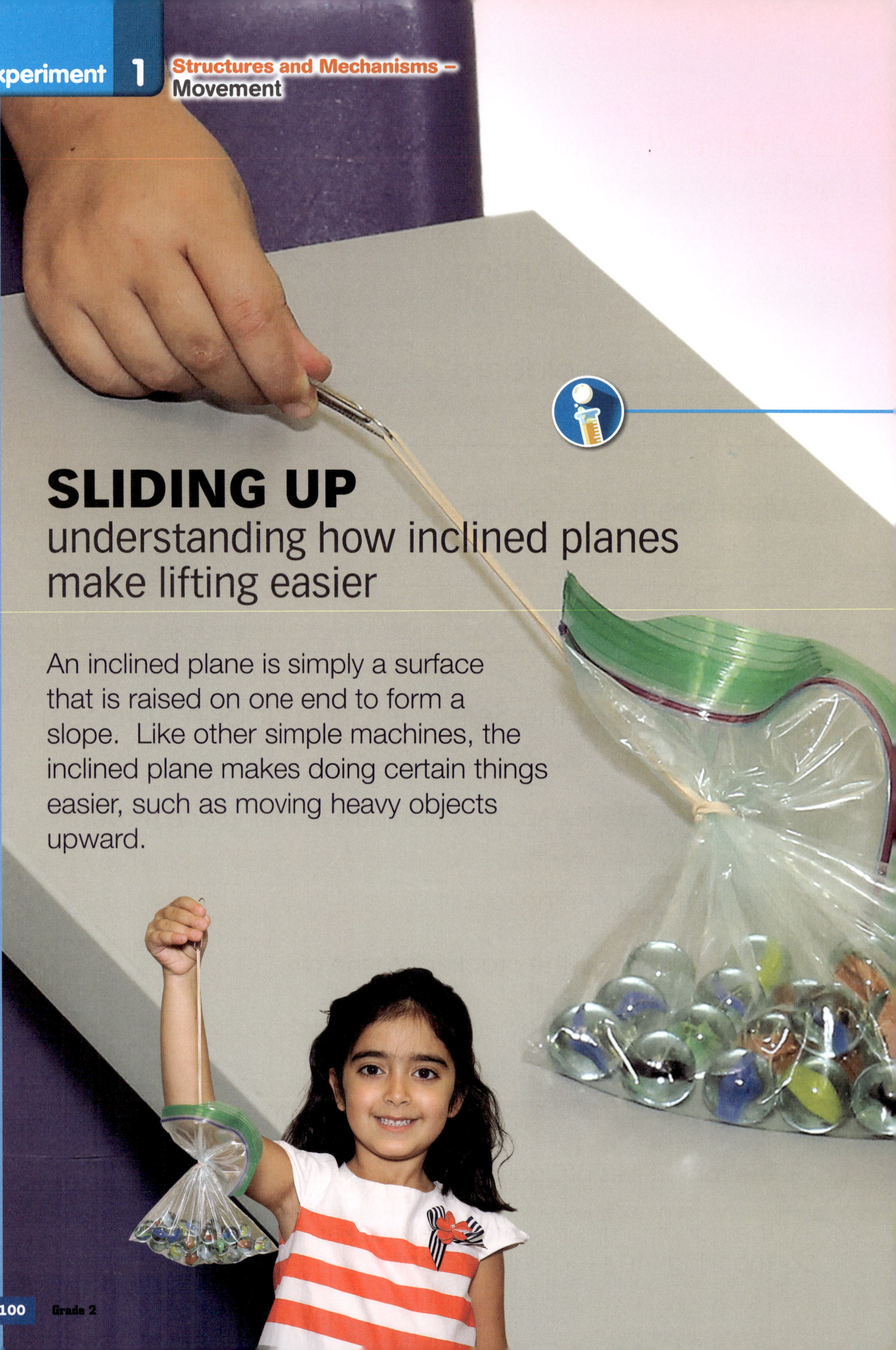

SLIDING UP

understanding how inclined planes make lifting easier

An inclined plane is simply a surface that is raised on one end to form a slope. Like other simple machines, the inclined plane makes doing certain things easier, such as moving heavy objects upward.

What you need:

a zipper bag

marbles

an elastic band

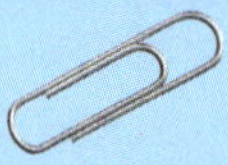

a paper clip

Difficulty:
●●●○○

Time needed:
30 minutes

In this experiment, you will see how an inclined plane makes moving objects upward easier.

You can use these for your inclined plane:

- a flat piece of cardboard
- a shelf from a bookshelf
- a rectangular cutting board
- a slide at the park

What to do:

1. Place some marbles into the zipper bag.
2. Tie the bag using the elastic band.
3. Loop the elastic band into the paper clip as shown.
4. Pinch the paper clip and lift the bag straight up. Notice how much the elastic band stretched.
5. Set up your inclined plane and set the bag at the bottom of the plane.
6. Pinch the paper clip and drag the bag up along the inclined plane. Make sure the bag always touches the inclined plane.
7. Did the elastic band stretch more when lifting the bag straight up or when dragging it along the inclined plane?
8. You can repeat this experiment using more marbles for more weight.

WHAT *just* happened?

In the experiment, you used the elastic band to measure how much force was needed to lift the bag. When you pulled the elastic band, it stretched. The more the elastic band stretched, the more force was needed to lift the bag.

When you dragged the bag up along the inclined plane, you might have observed that the elastic band stretched less compared to when you lifted the bag straight up, which means you exerted less force to do the same work. This is because of the inclined plane. An inclined plane is a simple machine that makes lifting easier by reducing the force needed to move an object upward. Therefore, in this experiment, with the support of the inclined plane, you did not need to apply as much force as when you lifted the bag without using an inclined plane.

STEM INQUIRY

- How does the number of marbles placed into the zipper bag affect the stretching of the elastic band?

- Ask someone to take photos when different numbers of the marbles are dragged. Compare the photos with fewer marbles to those with more marbles and examine the length of the elastic band in each. What do you find?
- Inclined planes are simple machines that are widely used in everyday applications. With the help of an adult, go online to find out where inclined planes are commonly used and what purposes they serve.

- Why is it important for inclined planes to have flat surfaces?

- If you want to weigh the marbles in the bag, what unit of measurement can you use?

Fun to know

Big Chute Marine Railway

Boats sometimes need to travel from one body of water to another. Normally this would take a lot of work but with simple machines, this process can be made easier. The Big Chute Marine Railway located in Ontario, Canada is a machine-powered inclined plane that is able to transport boats uphill over land from one body of water to another.

UP AND EASY

understanding how pulleys make lifting easier

A pulley is another simple machine that makes doing certain tasks easier. Like inclined planes, pulleys also make it easier to move heavy objects upward; however, pulleys do it differently.

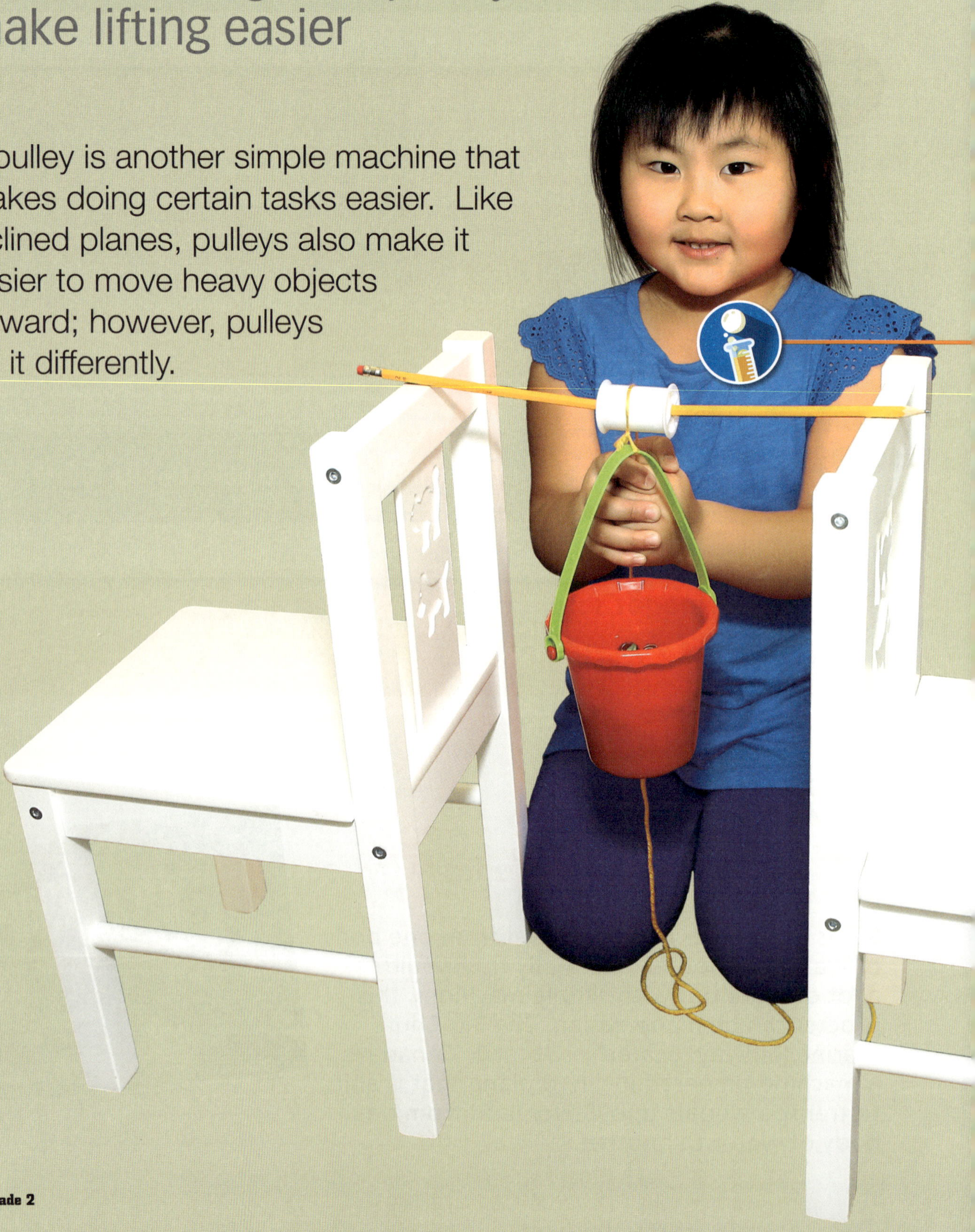

What you need:

string

2 pencils

a pail with a handle

an empty spool

15 marbles

Difficulty: ●●●○○

Time needed: 30 minutes

In this experiment, you will see how a pulley makes it easier to lift objects.

What to do:

Part 1

1. Place 15 marbles into the pail.
2. Tie one end of the string to the handle of the pail.
3. Try lifting the pail by pulling the string upward. Was it easy to lift it?

Part 1

Part 2

1. Insert the pencils into the spool.
2. Rest the two ends of the pencils between two edges (such as between two chairs or tables) with the spool hanging above ground.
3. With one end of the string tied to the pail, pass the other end over the spool.
4. Pull the other end of the string to lift the pail. Was it easier to lift it?

Part 2

WHAT *just* happened?

When you tried lifting the pail with the spool, you might have noticed that it felt easier compared to lifting it without the spool. However, the amount of force needed in both cases was actually the same. So why did it feel easier with the spool?

In the experiment, the spool acted as a pulley, which changed the direction of the force you exerted. Instead of pulling up, you pulled down the string to lift the pail. It is easier to pull something downward than upward because of gravity. Gravity is the force that pulls things toward the ground. When you pull something upward, you have to work against gravity. In contrast, when you pull something downward, gravity helps you, making it feel easier.

Therefore, by using the spool as a pulley and with gravity's assistance, it felt easier to lift the pail, even though the force needed was the same as lifting it directly upward.

STEM INQUIRY

- Where was the energy that moved the load with the pulley from?

- The pulley is a simple machine that is used all around us. Make a list of places where you can find pulleys. If needed, use the Internet with the help of an adult.

- Try changing the direction you pull the string. Does this affect the effort needed to move the pail?
- What will happen if you change the size of the spool used in this experiment?
- Use materials you can find around your home to make a small flagpole that has a pulley.

- Try adding more marbles to the pail. How many marbles could you pick up with the pulley?

Fun to know

Pulleys and Flags

Did you know there is a pulley that you see every day? The next time you are at school, take a closer look at the top of the flagpole. You might spot the pulley. The flag is attached to one end of the rope that runs through the pulley. By pulling the other end of the rope, the flag is able to move up the pole.

RAISE IT UP!

understanding how levers make work easier

Playing on a seesaw is so much fun. But did you know that the seesaw is actually a simple machine? Whether it is a seesaw, a shovel, nail clippers, or a bottle opener, all these objects are actually levers that can help us make our work easier.

What you need:

a large binder clip

a 12-in/30-cm long ruler

an elastic band

modeling clay

marbles

2 jar lids

Difficulty: ●●●○○

Time needed: 30 minutes

In this experiment, you will learn how levers make work easier.

STEM Note

A standard ruler is marked with measurements in both inches and centimeters, which are units used to measure lengths. The inch is a unit in the imperial system of measurement, while the centimeter belongs to the metric system. In fact, 1 inch is about 2.54 centimeters.

What to do:

1. Secure a jar lid on each end of the ruler with the modeling clay.
2. Remove the handles from the binder clip.
3. Attach the ruler to the binder clip using the elastic band as shown below, which is Setup A.

Setup A

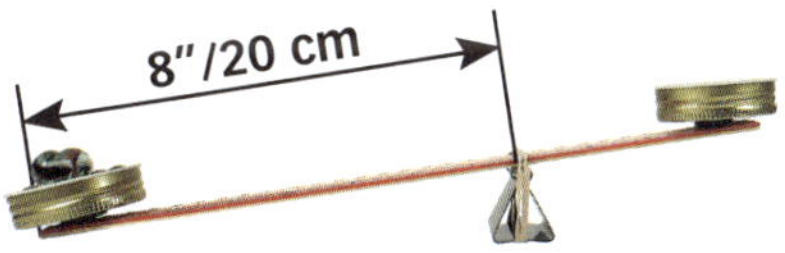

4. Put 8 marbles into the lid on the left. Then add marbles into the other lid one by one until the lid on the left is lifted. Record the number of marbles needed in the chart on the next page.
5. Repeat the experiment for Setups B and C on the next page.

My Record

Setup A	Setup B	Setup C
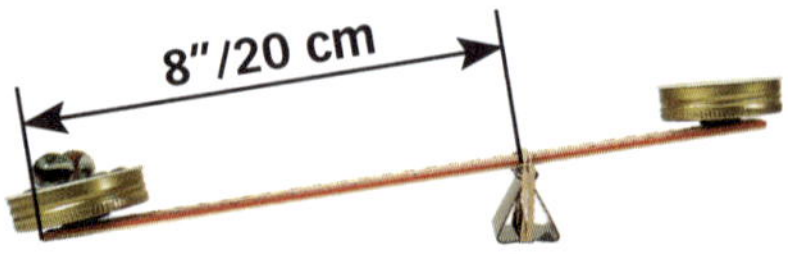	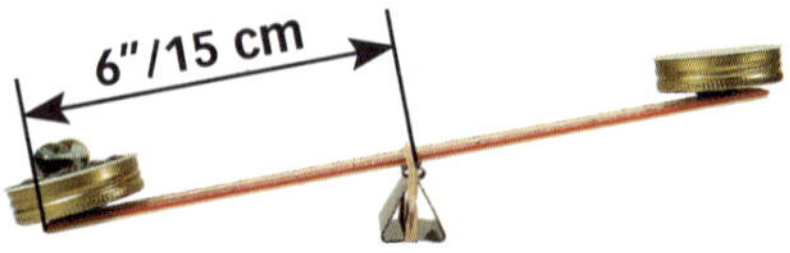	
______ marbles	______ marbles	______ marbles

WHAT *just* happened?

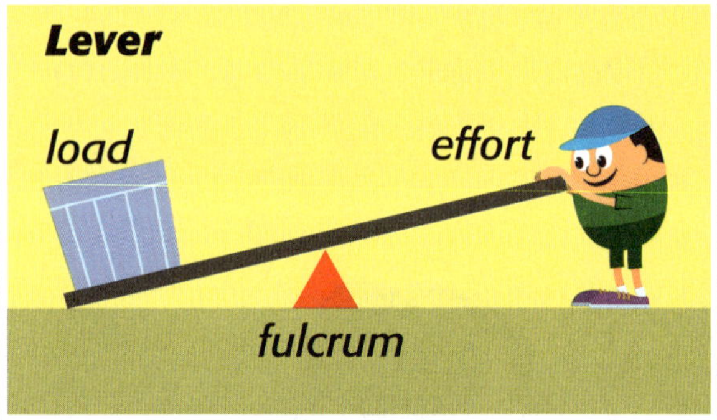

A lever contains three parts – a fulcrum, a load, and an effort. In the experiment, the binder clip was the fulcrum, the lid with eight marbles was the load, and the lid with the added marbles was the effort. In Setup A, you should have noticed that more than eight marbles were needed to lift the lid on the left, but in Setup C, fewer than eight marbles were needed. This is because the fulcrum was closer to the load in Setup C than in Setup A, so less effort was needed to lift the load. A lever is able to help us lift loads with less effort when the fulcrum is placed closer to the load.

STEM INQUIRY

- Why was the binder clip (without handles) suitable as a fulcrum for the experiment?

- What properties (e.g. weight, hardness, rigidity) should a lever have?
- How can levers be used in real-world applications, such as in construction and engineering, to make things work better?
- What should you consider when using levers, such as ensuring proper balance, avoiding overloading, and maintaining stability?

- If 6 marbles are in the load instead of 8 marbles, how many marbles do you think are needed to lift the load in Setups A, B, and C?

Fun to know

Lever in Hammers

When we think of hammers, we picture nails being pounded on with the blunt side of the hammer. But have you ever wondered what the other side is used for? It is actually a part of a lever. It comes in handy when nails need to be removed. To remove a nail, it must first be slipped between the two prongs of a hammer. Then the handle of the hammer must be pulled back. The force applied will then pull the nail out.

A SMART SPLITTER

understanding how wedges make work easier

We use many tools every day to make our lives easier. Consider the knife for example. A knife allows us to split, cut, and peel an apple quickly without much effort. Imagine trying to do all that work without a knife! It would be very difficult. So how does a knife make these kinds of tasks easier?

CAUTION!

Ask an adult to carve the pencil for you.

What you need:

2 unsharpened pencils

a box cutter

a bar of soap

Difficulty: ●●○○○

Time needed: 10 minutes

In this experiment, you will learn how wedges make it easier to get things done.

What to do:

1. Carve one of the unsharpened pencils with the box cutter to form a V-shape at the tip.
2. Place the bar of soap on a table.
3. Place the tip of the unsharpened pencil onto the soap and try to push it in. Pay attention to the amount of effort you needed.
4. Repeat Step 3 with the carved pencil.
5. Compare the difference in the effort needed.

STEM Note

The wooden casing and the core (a combination of graphite and clay) allow pencils to be sharpened easily. Pencils are classified into grades, with each grade indicating the hardness of the core. The most common grading scale ranges from 9H (hardest) to 9B (softest), with HB representing the middle point.

WHAT *just* happened?

You should have noticed that it was much easier to push the carved pencil into the bar of soap compared to the unsharpened pencil.

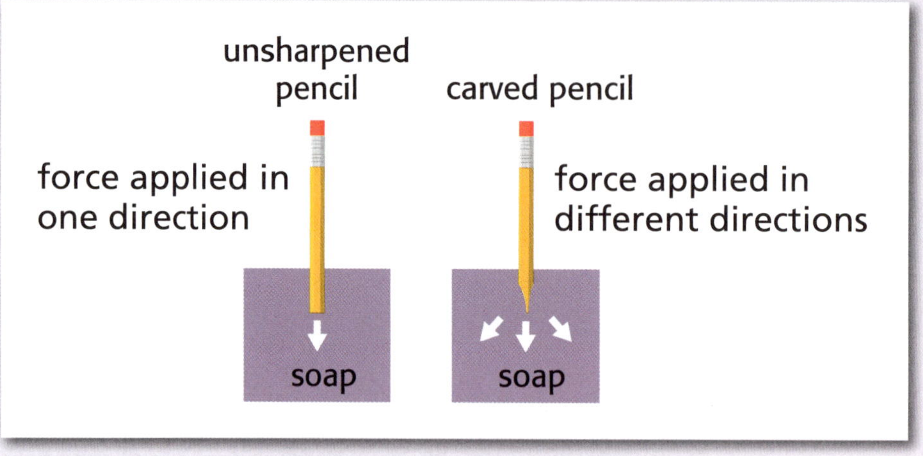

The tip of the carved pencil is shaped like a wedge. A wedge is wider at one end and tapers to a point at the other end. When you pushed the unsharpened pencil into the soap, the force was only applied in one direction. However, with the carved pencil, the force was spread in different directions: downward and to the left and right sides. By spreading the force, the effort needed to push the pencil into the soap was reduced. That is why it was easier to push the carved pencil into the soap compared to the unsharpened one.

STEM INQUIRY

- What do you think the difference in the result will be if the pencil is sharpened using a sharpener instead of being cut into a V-shape at the tip?
- Does the angle or position at which the pencil is held affect how easily it goes into the soap?

- Wedges are not only used for cutting but can also serve to hold things together. Do some research online with the help of an adult to find examples of wedges holding things together.

- How do the findings of this experiment relate to everyday cutting tools with different shapes or sharpness?
- How do you test the strength and durability of wedges?
- Find more wedges around your home and think about how these wedges are modified to perform different tasks. Be careful when you study them.

Fun to know

Pointy Wedges

Wedges are not only found on knives and axes. Pointy objects are wedges too! Forks and nails are examples of pointy wedges. Unlike flat wedges which primarily push materials to the left and right, pointy wedges push materials away in all directions.

ALL MACHINES COMBINED

understanding how simple machines work together

Many machines today are a combination of different simple machines. For example, a pair of scissors consists of two blades, which are wedges. These wedges are fastened together to form a lever that can make cutting easier. By combining different simple machines, we can do things that no single simple machine can do alone.

What you need:

a large box

tape

marbles in a bag, tied with a string

a clothespin

modeling clay

a long ruler

a binder clip

a pencil

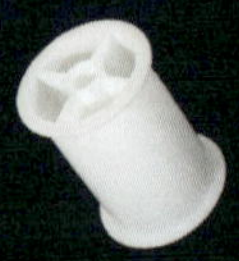
a spool

a pin

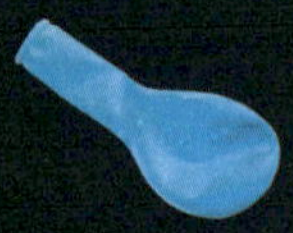
a balloon

Difficulty:

●●●●●

Time needed:
1 hour

In this experiment, you will build an interesting machine using different simple machines and see how they work together to get something done.

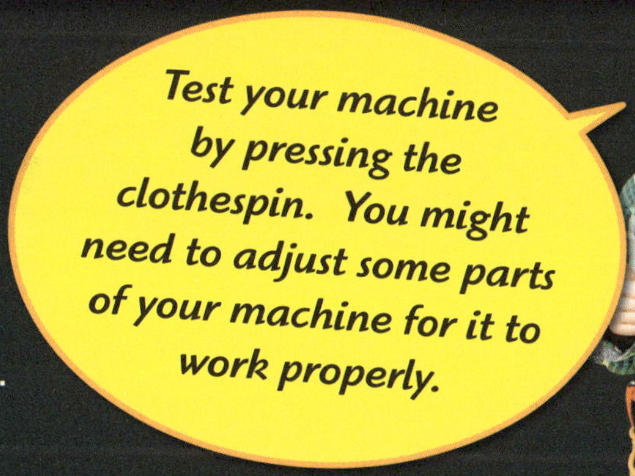

What to do:

1. Poke a hole through the box and insert the pencil into it.
2. Place the spool onto the pencil.
3. Tape down the clothespin.
4. Hang the bag of marbles over the spool and secure the other end of the string to the clothespin to keep it hanging.
5. Remove the handles from the binder clip and tape it down.
6. Place the ruler over the binder clip to make a lever. Make sure one end of the ruler is directly below the bag of marbles.
7. Secure the pin with its point facing upward on the other end of the ruler with modeling clay.
8. Inflate the balloon and tape it on the side of the box above the pin. Make sure the pin can reach the balloon when the lever is raised.

WHAT *just* happened?

It might have required some adjustments, but once your machine was put together, it must have been exciting to see it pop the balloon when you pushed the clothespin!

Sometimes, a single simple machine may not be enough to accomplish the tasks we want. That is when the power of combining different simple machines comes into play. By putting them together, we can do a great variety of things.

In the case of the experiment, you combined a pulley, a lever, and a wedge. Normally, just pushing a clothespin cannot pop a balloon. However, by using these different machines together, you created a unique setup where pushing a clothespin could successfully pop a balloon.

STEM INQUIRY

- Describe in detail how the components in the setup worked together to pop the balloon.
- What characteristics does the spool have that make it a pulley?
- Name the objects used as the components of the lever. What are the load and effort?

- A machine that consists of two or more simple machines is called a compound machine. With the help of an adult, research online and find examples of compound machines around your home. Identify the simple machines that make up these compound machines.

- What adjustments did you make to the setup to achieve the desired result?
- How can the information you learned from this experiment be applied to real-life scenarios or the development of practical machines and devices?

- Will adding or reducing the number of marbles in the bag change the result? If so, what changes will each modification make?
- Try this experiment again by changing the position of the fulcrum (the binder clip) as shown below.

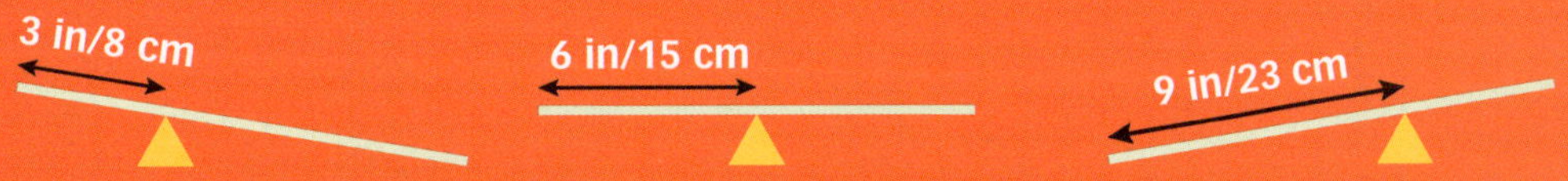

Which works the best?

Section 3

Matter and Energy

1 Liquids

Some liquids are from nature and some are human-made. In this unit, you will identify different liquids and examine the properties that make them liquids.

After completing this unit, you will

- be able to identify liquids.
- understand that some liquids are from nature and some are human-made.
- understand the properties of liquids.

Vocabulary

liquid: can flow; can be poured; takes the shape of its container

clear: easy to see through

opaque: impossible to see through

property: quality of something

Extension

Within our bodies, there is a lot of liquid! Our blood is liquid, and its property of being able to flow helps move nutrients and oxygen through our bodies.

Can you think of other examples of liquids in our bodies?

A. Look at the liquids. Determine whether they are from nature or are human-made. Write the letters.

Liquids

From Nature

Human-made

B. Identify the liquids. Check ✔ the circles. Then circle the correct words.

1.

2. Properties of Liquids

- **can / cannot** flow
- **takes / does not take** the shape of the container it is in
- **can / cannot** be poured

C. **Check ✔ the properties of each liquid. Then read what each child says to determine which of the liquids he or she is talking about. Write the answers on the lines.**

chocolate milk

Properties:

- ◯ clear
- ◯ opaque
- ◯ runny
- ◯ greasy

ketchup

Properties:

- ◯ clear
- ◯ opaque
- ◯ runny
- ◯ greasy

cooking oil

Properties:

- ◯ clear
- ◯ opaque
- ◯ runny
- ◯ greasy

This liquid is greasy. My dad uses it to fry chicken.

1. ____________________

I love to add this to my fries. It is not runny compared to many liquids.

2. ____________________

This tastes really good. It is very runny so I had to be careful when pouring it into my cup.

3. ____________________

2 Solids

Solids can be from nature or human-made. In this unit, you will identify different solids and examine the properties that make them solids.

After completing this unit, you will

- be able to identify solids.
- understand that some solids are from nature and some are human-made.
- understand the properties of solids.

Vocabulary

solid: has its own shape that does not change easily

granular: looking like small grains

Extension

Spiderwebs might look delicate, but these solids that spiders create are amazing. The threads in spiderwebs are considered very strong for how thin they are – even when compared to steel! They are also incredibly elastic, meaning that they can be stretched a lot without breaking. Spiders use their silk to catch prey, make nests, and even to make "parachutes" to float through the air.

A. Determine whether each solid is human-made or from nature. Write the letters.

A

B

C

D

E
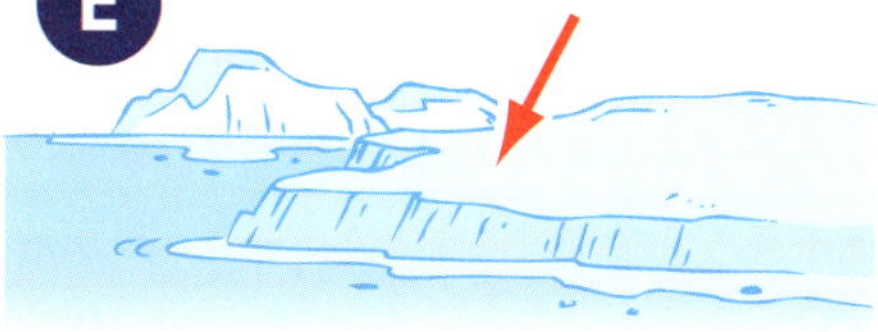

F

Human-made

From Nature

B. Identify and name two things that are solids in each picture. Then check ✔ the properties of solids.

1.

____

____

2.

____

____

3.

____

____

4.

____

____

Properties of Solids

Ⓐ can be poured

Ⓑ has its own shape

Ⓒ shape does not change easily

Ⓓ may be spilled

C. Circle the correct descriptions for each solid. Then do what the child says.

1. sponge

hard	clear
opaque	soft
light	granular

2. dried beans

soft	granular
clear	smooth
rough	opaque

3. brick

soft	rough
heavy	clear
hard	granular

4. glass

smooth	soft
granular	clear
hard	opaque

5.

Give an example of a solid that is...

a. opaque and granular.

____

b. soft and smooth.

____

3 Liquids and Solids (1)

Liquids and solids have unique properties. In this unit, you will identify different liquids and solids. You will also review and compare their properties.

After completing this unit, you will

- be able to determine whether objects are liquids or solids.
- understand the differences between the properties of liquids and solids.

Vocabulary

matter: everything around us; can be animals, objects, and water

form: the way in which something appears

Extension

Water is matter that is very important for our survival. Whether it is in liquid form or solid form, water is useful to us. For example, we wash our clothes with water in liquid form and skate on water in solid form.

Think of what we use water for in our lives to see how important water is to us.

	Art	Sports
Water (in liquid form)		
Water (in solid form)		

A. A liquid and a solid are indicated in each picture. Write "L" for liquid and "S" for solid.

1.

2.

3.

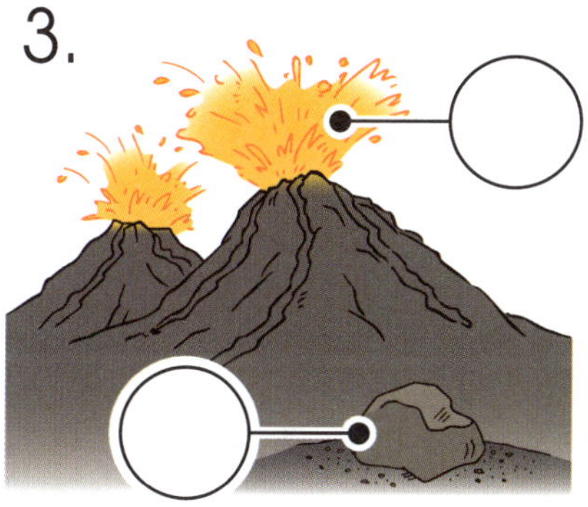

4.

5.

6.

B. Write "liquid" or "solid" to tell what each verse is about. Then sort the things into the correct groups. Write the letters in the circles.

1.

It has a shape

It has a size

It is hard to change

Before your eyes

It is a ____________ .

◯ ◯ ◯ ◯

2.

It flows, it pours

It's thick, it's thin

It takes the shape

Of whatever it's in

It is a ____________ .

◯ ◯ ◯ ◯

C. Read the paragraph. Describe the liquids and solids in the pictures with the descriptive words from the paragraph. Then answer the question.

Different liquids and solids have different properties. Cooking oil is greasy, clear, and runny when it is poured. Paint is sticky, opaque, and thick when it is poured. A sponge is soft and light to pick up. Uncooked rice is hard, and its many similar, small pieces make it granular.

1.

____

____

____

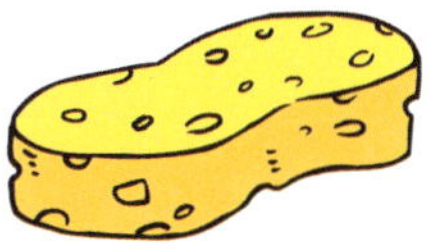

____

____

____

____

2. Give an example of

a. a solid that is opaque and light.

____

b. a liquid that is clear and sticky.

____

4 Liquids and Solids (2)

Different liquids and solids have different properties. In this unit, you will see how liquids and solids interact with other liquids and solids.

After completing this unit, you will

- know that liquids and solids interact in different ways.
- know that only some solids are buoyant.

Vocabulary

absorb: soak up liquid

dissolve: become part of a liquid

buoyant: able to float

repel: not allow through

Extension

Mixing some liquids – tea and honey, for example – is harmless. When cooking, adding oil to hot water is okay, too. But adding water to hot oil will cause splattering or, in some cases, even an explosion! This is because oil can get much hotter than water. So when drops of water come into contact with hot oil, the water will heat up almost instantly, causing it to splatter.

A. Fill in the blanks with the correct words to describe the pictures.

absorbs **dissolves** **buoyant** **repels**

1. 

Ice floats on water.

Ice is ______________ .

2. 

Water slides off the plastic glove.

The glove ______________ water.

3. 

The towel soaks up the spill.

The towel ______________ the spill.

4. 

The salt disappears in the soup.

The salt ______________ in the soup.

B. Write the letters in the bucket to show whether the items are buoyant. Then give examples of your own.

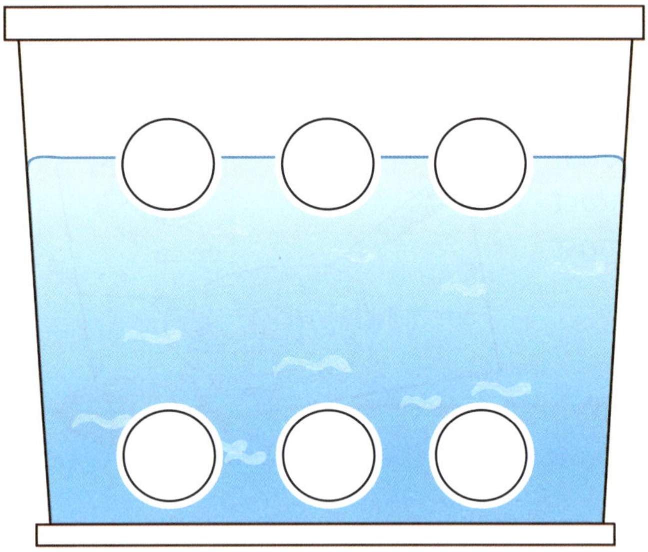

An Item That Floats: ______________________

An Item That Sinks: ______________________

C. Determine whether each item absorbs or repels liquids. Fill in the blanks.

1.

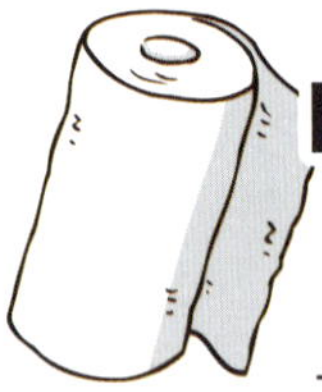

paper towel

__________ liquids

2.

plastic wrap

__________ liquids

3. fabric table cloth

__________ liquids

4. rain jacket

__________ liquids

5. sponge

__________ liquids

D. Read the paragraph. Then fill in the blanks with the correct words to describe the situations.

There are different ways in which liquids and solids interact with other liquids and solids. For example, two solids do not mix with each other. But when two liquids are put together and stirred, they may mix or they may not.

do not mix
absorbs
dissolves
sinks
mix
floats

Solid and Solid

- blocks and marbles

  ____

Liquid and Liquid

- oil and water

  ____

- lemon juice and water

  ____

Liquid and Solid

- sand in water

  ____

- cork in water

  ____

- sock in water

  ____

- sugar in water

  ____

5 Changes of State

Water has special properties. It can be a liquid or a solid. In this unit, you will learn that water, in both its liquid and its solid forms, plays an important role in our lives.

After completing this unit, you will

- know that water can be a liquid or a solid.
- understand what freezing and melting are.
- understand what a change of state is.

vocabulary

freeze: (of a liquid) turn into a solid

melt: (of a solid) turn into a liquid

Extension

Freezing juice into ice pops, melting butter on hot toast – changes of state seem harmless. However, melting glaciers have become a problem. A glacier is a huge block of ice that can be found in cold regions. As Earth's temperature rises, glaciers melt into liquid water. This change of state not only reduces living space for some animals like polar bears, but it also leads to flooding in some coastal regions.

A. Unscramble the letters to find out the states of water the boy is talking about. Then write the states of water the pictures show.

1. *We can drink it.*

a. ____________
qliudi

I add this to make my drink cold.

b. ____________
iosld

2. 

ice cap ____________

3. 

____

4. 

____

B. Write the state of each thing. Circle the correct word. Then check ✔ the circle if the state is changed or cross it out ✘ if it is not.

Change of State

1.  → 

Ice **melts** / **freezes** when heated.

2. 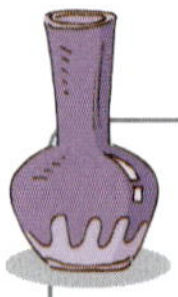 → 

Solids remain solid when **melted** / **broken** .

3.  → 

Jelly becomes solid when **heated** / **cooled** .

4.  → 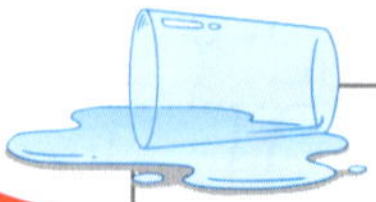

Liquids remain liquid when **spilled** / **frozen** .

C. Fill in the blanks with the correct words.

melts	**freezes**	**solid**	**liquid**	**water**	**ice**

1. 

Change of State:

liquid → ____________

The water ____________ and becomes ____________ .

2. 

Change of State:

solid → ____________

The ice ____________ and becomes liquid ____________ .

D. Look at the change of state of water in each picture. Fill in the blanks.

1. 

Water in a skating rink ____________
melts/freezes

from ____________ to ____________ .

2. 

The snowman in the sun ____________
melts/freezes

from ____________ to ____________ .

6 Safety with Liquids and Solids

Many liquids and solids are important in our lives, but we must handle some of them with care. In this unit, you will learn how to be as safe as possible with liquids and solids.

After completing this unit, you will

- understand that there are some basic ways to be safe around liquids and solids.
- know the meanings of some hazard symbols.
- know that some changes of state of liquids and solids can have impacts on us.

This sign tells us that the solution in this container can burn your skin. We should handle it carefully.

Vocabulary

waterproof: does not let water through

hazard: a source of danger

raincoat and boots (waterproof)

Extension

Liquids need containers, and good containers keep liquids from spilling or leaking. For this reason, containers must be waterproof – an important property for avoiding leaks. Besides being waterproof, some containers are made with special locks on their caps to keep you safe from the liquids or solids that are inside.

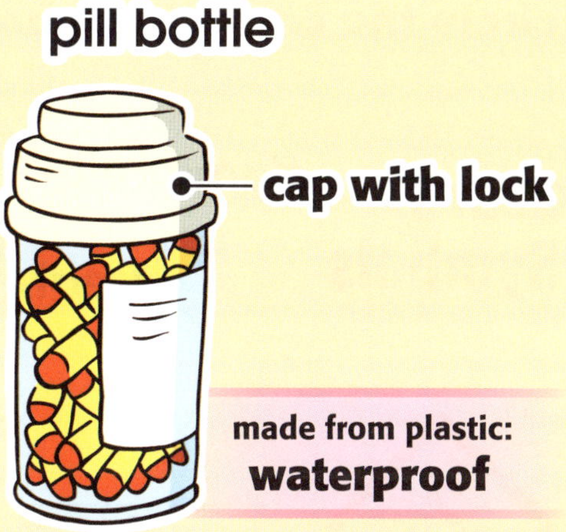

A. Fill in the blanks to show what to do to be safe around liquids and solids that need to be handled with care.

How to Be Safe around Liquids and Solids

children
containers
spills
mix
warnings

- Clean up ____________________ right away.
- Read the ____________________ on containers.
- Do not ____________________ cleaning liquids.
- Keep cleaning products and medicines in their original ____________________ .
- Store them out of reach of ____________________ .

B. Label the hazard symbols and complete the descriptions. Then circle the correct symbols.

Hazard Symbols

flammable explosive poisonous corrosive

heated swallowed burn fire

1.  ____________ (It may explode if it is punctured or ____________ .)

2.  ____________ (It will catch ____________ easily if it is near heat.)

3.  ____________ (It may ____________ skin or eyes upon contact.)

4.  ____________ (It may cause illness or death if ____________ .)

5. 

6. 

C. Read the paragraph. Then answer the questions.

We use water in our daily lives, and it affects many of our activities. When water changes state, it can also affect what we can do. For example, when rain turns to freezing rain, it can become dangerous to do basic things such as driving or walking. What could happen in each situation below if a change in state occurs?

1. If the ice on a lake begins to melt, will it still be safe to skate? Explain.

____

____

____

____

2. If the rain turns to snow, will it still be safe to drive? Explain.

____

____

____

____

MIXING THEM
understanding solid and liquid interactions

Liquids and solids are all around us. We often mix them to make things we need. We make cookies, for example, by mixing flour (solid) and egg (liquid); we make chocolate milk by mixing chocolate syrup (liquid) and milk (liquid). But not all solids and liquids can mix. So what solids and liquids mix? Which ones do not mix?

What you need:

rice

salt

sand

modeling clay

water

milk

oil

jars

What to do:

1. Before mixing the materials in each pair below, predict whether the two materials will mix or not.

solid and solid

solid and liquid

liquid and liquid

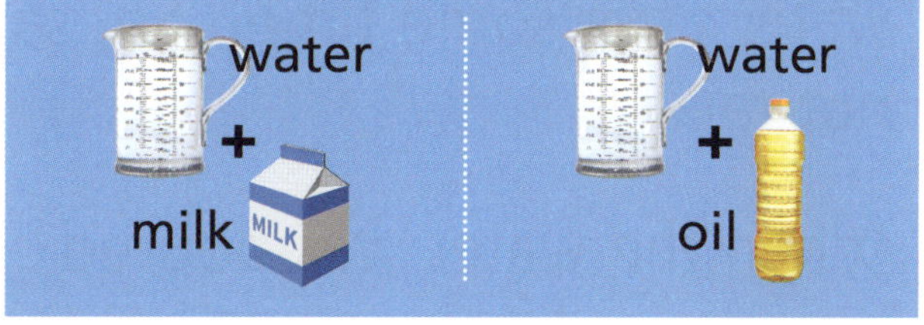

2. Mix each pair of materials. Observe.

Difficulty:

●●●○○

Time needed:
15 minutes

In this experiment, you will mix different solids and liquids to see how they interact with each other.

STEM Note

Solids and liquids are measured using different units. The ounce (oz) and gram (g) are used to measure the weight of solids, while the fluid ounce (fl oz) and liter (L) are used to measure the volume of liquids.

WHAT *just* happened?

You should have observed the following:

1 The two materials in each group, no matter how hard you mixed them, were still visible. However, there are some solids that do mix.

2 When you mixed the salt and the water, the salt seemed to disappear because it dissolved in the water. So, salt and water mix. For the sand and the water, the sand stayed separated from the water after some time. So, sand and water do not mix.

3 When the water was poured into the milk, the two liquids mixed and it was impossible to see each material separately in the mixture. As for the water and the oil, they remained in separate layers even after you stirred them. So, water and oil do not mix.

You can also try other materials such as sugar, flour, and syrup to see how solids and liquids interact.

STEM INQUIRY

- When mixing the solids, do you think using different quantities of each solid will change the result?
- Other than salt, what other solids can also dissolve in water?
- Do you think stirring will affect the mixing or separation of solids and liquids?
- If less oil is used, do you think it will mix with the water?

- A centrifuge is a machine used to separate substances. How does a centrifuge work? What are some common fields in which it is used? With the help of an adult, do some research online to find out.

- How do you think temperature affects the mixing of solids and liquids? Does it help them mix better or make it harder for them to mix?

Fun to know

Detergent – a Mediator

Some materials can bond together other substances that usually do not mix. Dishwashing detergent is a good example. Oil and grease normally cannot be washed away with water since they do not mix. However, once dishwashing detergent is added, it helps the oil and water bond together so that oil and grease can be washed away with water, leaving dishes squeaky clean.

FRIEND OR FOE?

how water and oil interact

Different solids and liquids can interact with each other by dissolving or mixing together. However, this does not happen all the time. This experiment will show you an example of what happens when two substances do not interact.

What will happen?

What you need:

water

foam

a sponge

vegetable oil

cotton balls

paper towels

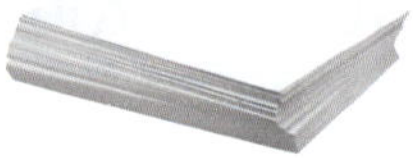
paper

a jar with a lid

STEM Note

Vegetable oil comes from plants and is derived from seeds, nuts, or fruits. Some commonly used vegetable oils are canola oil, olive oil, sunflower oil, corn oil, peanut oil, and coconut oil.

Difficulty:

●●●○○

Time needed:
30 minutes

In this experiment, you will learn how water and oil interact and the difficulty in separating them.

What to do:

1. Fill the jar with water while leaving some space at the top for the oil.
2. Pour the vegetable oil into the jar until the jar is nearly full. Observe.
3. Close the jar with the lid tightly secured. Shake the jar to mix the oil and the water. Observe.
4. Next, use the different materials to try to soak up the oil from the water. Did each material do a good job of soaking up the oil?
5. Record your observations in the chart on the next page.

My Record

Material	Observation
Cotton Ball	
Foam	
Paper Towel	
Sponge	
Paper	

WHAT *just* happened?

You should have noticed that the water and the oil did not mix together or dissolve, even after shaking the jar.

Unlike separating solids such as popcorns and nuts, liquids are difficult to separate. To separate water and oil, you can soak up one of the liquids from the other. But not all materials are equally effective in absorbing oil. For example, the paper towel did a better job of soaking up the oil compared to the foam.

STEM INQUIRY

- What other liquids do you think cannot mix together or dissolve? Try this experiment with other liquids such as rubbing alcohol, corn syrup, and liquid soap.
- Do you think other states of matter (gases and solids) have this problem?
- Do you think there are any solids that can dissolve in water? Give some real-world examples to support your hypothesis.

- As we learned in this experiment, oil and water do not mix. Can we use this information to help some items repel water?
- What other methods can you use to separate oil and water from each other?

- What tools can you use to measure the liquids in this experiment? What is the best unit of measurement to use?

Fun to know

Oily Hair

Oil is an essential resource we rely on to power cars and machines. However, extracting oil can be messy and sometimes disastrous when accidental spills occur, especially in the ocean.

During a serious oil spill in 2010, many people got involved by donating their hair! Surprisingly, hair proved to be a good oil sponge. Thanks to the hair of many donors, the cleanup of the spill went much faster.

THE POWER OF HOT WATER

understanding that temperature affects how materials interact

Water is commonly used for cleaning purposes. But when it comes to oil, water cannot get the job done well because they do not mix with each other. But what if hot water is used instead?

What you need:

2 jars

2 identical spoons

oil

water

paper towels

a pen

STEM Note

Water temperatures for everyday activities can vary based on personal preference. Below are some general guidelines:

- for drinking: 68 – 77°F (20 – 25°C)
- for showering: 100 – 104°F (38 – 40°C)
- for swimming pools: 78 – 82°F (26 – 28°C)

Difficulty: ●○○○○

Time needed:
2 hours

In this experiment, you will discover that oil behaves differently in hot water and in cold water.

What to do:

1. Fill one of the jars with water and leave it in the fridge for at least an hour.
2. Ask an adult for help to fill the other jar with the same amount of hot water from the faucet.
3. Place the two jars on the table.
4. Coat the two spoons with an equal amount of oil.
5. Put one spoon into each jar and gently stir for 30 seconds. Take the spoon out of the jar.
6. Wipe the spoon that was stirred in the cold water with a sheet of paper towel. Then label the sheet "cold water."
7. Repeat Step 6 for the spoon in the hot water. Label the sheet "hot water."
8. Allow time for both sheets of paper towels to dry.

WHAT *just* happened?

You should have noticed that the paper towel labeled "cold water" had more oil stains on it compared to the one labeled "hot water." This is the result of hot water being better than cold water at removing the oil from the spoon.

When you used hot water to wash the spoon, the hot water heated up the oil on the spoon, making it more fluid. This means the oil became more runny and thinner and therefore easier to be washed away.

On the other hand, when you used cold water, the oil was not heated up, so it stayed thick and sticky, making it harder to be removed. That is why you saw more oil stains on the paper towel labeled "cold water."

This experiment shows us the power of hot water when it comes to cleaning. Hot water can make substances, such as oil, more fluid and loosen up the dirt to make washing easier.

- Do you think the amount of oil on the spoons will affect the results of this experiment?
- How does the length of time that hot or cold water is applied affect how well it can remove oil stains?
- Repeat this experiment but add a small amount of liquid soap in both jars after Step 3. Did this change the results of your experiment?
- Repeat the experiment using different types of oil (e.g. olive oil and coconut oil). Did they all appear more fluid in hot water than cold water?
- Do you know any other substances that might be difficult to clean with cold water but easier to remove with hot water?

- Does hot water work equally well in removing oil stains from various surfaces like plastic, glass, and fabric?
- According to this experiment, hot water does a better job at breaking down oil than cold water. Does it help engineers design tools and machines for cleaning household items, such as dishwashers and washing machines? How do they work?

- Use a thermometer to measure the temperature of the water. With the help of an adult, repeat this experiment with warm water. Was there any change when warm water was used? Compare the sizes of the oil stains left by using different water temperatures.

SALTY ICE

understanding that properties of materials can change through interactions

What you need:

				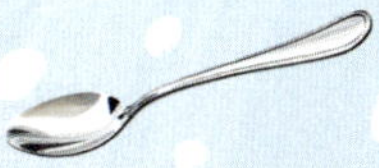
an ice cube tray	water	salt	2 plates	a spoon

Carol was ready to go to school, but the snowstorm the night before had left the walkway very slippery. So Carol helped shovel the walkway while her dad sprinkled salt to melt the ice and snow. How does salt do this?

Difficulty:
●●○○○

Time needed:
6 hours

In this experiment, you will learn about how ice interacts with salt.

What to do:

1. Add water to the ice cube tray and put it in the freezer. Wait for the water to freeze. (You may add a few drops of the food coloring to the water to help make the result more obvious.)

2. Put 3 ice cubes on each plate.

Transfer the ice cubes to the plates quickly to avoid melting them in your hands.

3. Sprinkle a spoonful of salt onto the ice cubes on one of the plates.

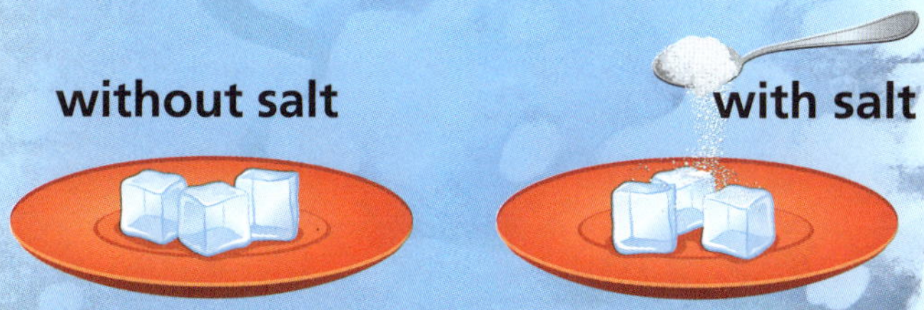

4. Observe and see which ice cubes melt first.

WHAT *just* happened?

During the experiment, you might have noticed that the ice cubes with salt melted faster than the ones without salt. This happened because salt lowered the melting point of ice.

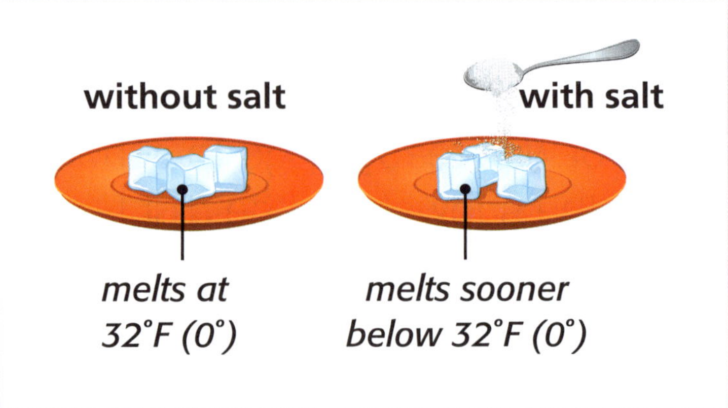

Normally, ice starts melting when the temperature reaches 32˚F (0˚C). However, when you added salt to the ice, something magical occurred – the salt actually lowered the temperature at which the ice melts. This means that the ice started melting at a temperature below 32˚F (0˚C), its normal melting point, making the ice begin melting sooner.

The effect of salt on ice makes it useful in winter. Salt is often spread on roads and pavements to melt the ice faster and sooner, making the surfaces safer for driving and walking.

STEM INQUIRY

- For the ice cubes with salt added, did you notice that the areas where the salt touched the ice tended to melt faster than other parts?

- Road salt is used to make our roads safer during the winter. Sea salt is used for food seasoning. What else is salt used for? With the help of an adult, do some research to find out.
- Explore the environmental impacts of using road salt to melt ice and find more eco-friendly alternatives for this purpose.

- Salt is not the only substance that can lower the melting point of ice; sugar can too. For road safety, why do you think sugar is not used instead to melt ice and snow?

- Try the experiment again and time how long it takes each plate of ice cubes to melt completely. How much more time was needed for the ice cubes without salt to melt?

Fun to know

Keeping Our Roads Safe

Walking and driving can be difficult and even dangerous during the snowy season. The roads often become slippery due to the snow and ice. To keep roads safe, our government sends out not only snowplows to clear snow, but also sand trucks to spread sand for traction and salt trucks to spread salt for speeding up the melting process.

WATER IN LAYERS

understanding how the density of water and temperature are related

Building layer cakes is fun and simple. All you have to do is start with a layer of cake and add a layer of frosting alternately. It is easy to layer solids, but how about liquids? Is it possible to create layers with liquid water? Try the experiment to see.

What you need:

red and blue food coloring

2 small identical jars

water

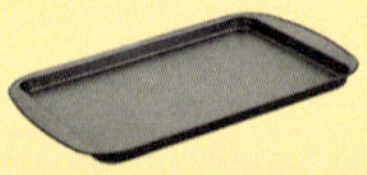
a baking sheet

a thin piece of cardboard

The cardboard must be larger than the openings of the jars.

STEM Note

Density is a measure of how tightly packed something is, which helps us find out if something feels heavy or light for its size.

CAUTION!

Ask an adult for help with hot water.

Difficulty: ●●●○○

Time needed:
1 hour

In this experiment, you will learn that temperature affects the density of water.

What to do:

1. Fill one jar with cold water and add a few drops of the blue food coloring.
2. With the help of an adult, fill the other jar with hot tap water and add a few drops of the red food coloring.
3. Put both jars of water on the baking sheet.
4. Cover the opening of the red jar with the cardboard.
5. While holding the red jar and cardboard in place, carefully turn the red jar upside down and rest it onto the blue jar to avoid spilling any water as shown in Setup 1.
6. Have someone hold onto both jars while you slowly and carefully pull out the cardboard. Then observe.
7. Repeat Steps 1 to 6 but place the blue jar onto the red jar instead as shown in Setup 2.

WHAT *just* happened?

When water is heated, it expands and becomes less dense. Therefore, hotter water tends to rise while colder, denser water sinks.

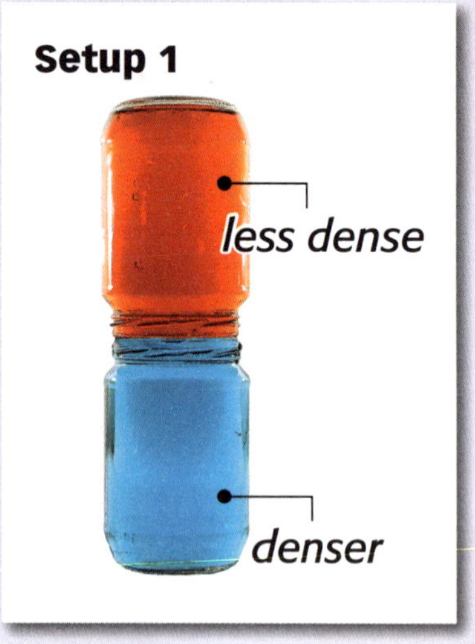

For Setup 1, you should have noticed that no mixing happened – both layers of colored water stayed where they were with hot red water floating over the cold blue water. This is because the hot water was less dense, so it stayed on top.

Conversely, mixing happened instantly and created purple water in Setup 2. This is because the hot red water was less dense and rose while the cold blue water was denser and sank.

- What is the purpose of using different colors for each jar?
- If you leave the hot water and cold water from Setup 1 out for longer, do you think they will eventually mix together?
- In Setup 2, do you think the mixing will be more or less obvious if the cold water is colder and the hot water is hotter?

- Are there energy-efficient technologies or systems that can optimize the heating or cooling process?

- How can we change the cardboard to make a better seal between the two jars?

- If the hot water from the tap is at 113°F (45°C) and the cold water is at 59°F (15°C), what do you think the approximate temperature will be when they are fully mixed together?

Fun to know

How Water Boils

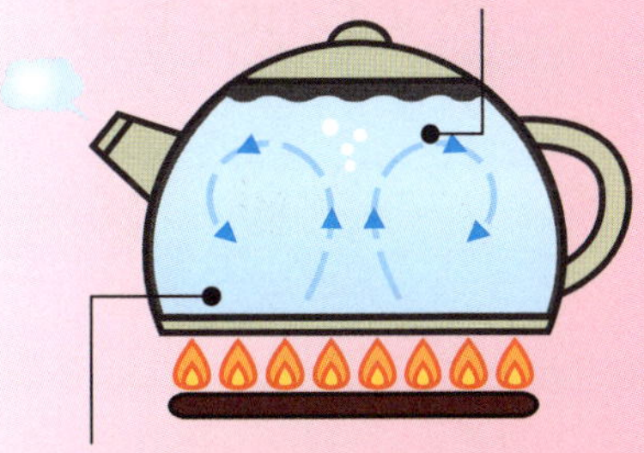

At first glance, you might think that the water in a kettle is sitting idle as it is being heated but, in fact, it is constantly on the move! The water at the bottom of the kettle is closer to the cooktop, so it heats up faster than the water at the top. As the water gets hotter and less dense, it rises to the top, while the now cooler water at the top sinks to the bottom. So rather than sitting idle, water in a kettle is in a cycle of rising and sinking as it reaches its boiling point.

FREEZING SOLIDS

exploring the properties of liquids when you freeze them

There are many different types of liquids in a kitchen. Water, oil, and honey are common liquids that we use for cooking and eating. Without them, we know that our food will not taste as delicious. But have you ever wondered what happens to these liquids when you freeze them?

What you need:

honey

water

oil

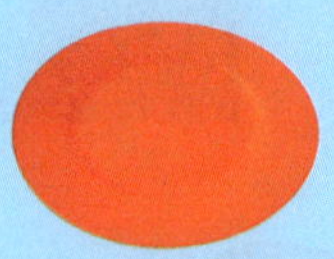
a plate

3 transparent cups

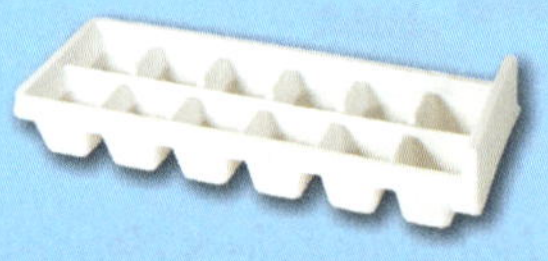
an ice cube tray

Wash the cups before the experiment so that you can still use the liquids in them after you are done.

What to do:

1. Fill each cell of the ice cube tray with different liquids – water, oil, and honey.
2. Leave the ice cube tray in the freezer overnight.
3. Fill one cup with water, another with oil, and the third with honey.
4. Take out the cubes and place them on the plate.
5. Do the observations below. Compare the solids and circle the best descriptions in the chart on the next page.

Difficulty: ●●○○○

Time needed: 2 days

In this experiment, you will investigate and compare the properties of water, oil, and honey when you freeze them.

Observations

- Touch each type of cube. Which one is the hardest?
- Are the cubes transparent (all light can pass through), translucent (some light can pass through), or opaque (no light can pass through)?
- Put each cube into the cup with its liquid form. Observe whether it floats or sinks.

My Record

	Water	Oil	Honey
Hardness	hard harder hardest	hard harder hardest	hard harder hardest
Transparency	transparent translucent opaque	transparent translucent opaque	transparent translucent opaque

WHAT *just* happened?

You should have noticed that water, oil, and honey have different properties when you freeze them. The ice cube, for instance, was translucent and seemed to be the hardest among the three cubes. The oil cube was opaque. The honey cube was transparent and it was not completely frozen because the temperature in most home freezers was not low enough to freeze honey. You can also see that both oil and honey cubes were not floating in their liquids. Water is special because, unlike most other liquids, its solid state is less dense than its liquid state. Since matter that is less dense floats on denser matter, ice always floats in water.

STEM INQUIRY

- Place the oil and the honey cubes in a glass of cold water. Does their buoyancy change?
- What are some ways you can describe the substances that were used in this experiment (water, oil, and honey)?

- With the help of an adult, find the definition of the words "buoyancy" and "transparency." How do you use these terms to describe different types of matter?

- Are the ice cubes in two- or three-dimensional shapes? What is the name of the shape?
- Use a ruler to take some measurements of the cubes. Repeat your measurements three times at 5-minute intervals and record your results in a chart like the one below. Were there any changes? If so, what caused these changes?

Measurements of Cubes

Time	Water Cube			Oil Cube			Honey Cube		
	Length	Width	Height	Length	Width	Height	Length	Width	Height

Section 4

Earth and Space Systems

1 What Is Air?

We cannot see air, but we know it surrounds us. In this unit, you will learn about air and some of its properties.

After completing this unit, you will

- learn that air takes up space.
- know that air has mass.
- know that air can make things move.

Vocabulary

air: a gas that surrounds us; we feel it as wind

mass: amount of matter that something has; can be measured by a scale

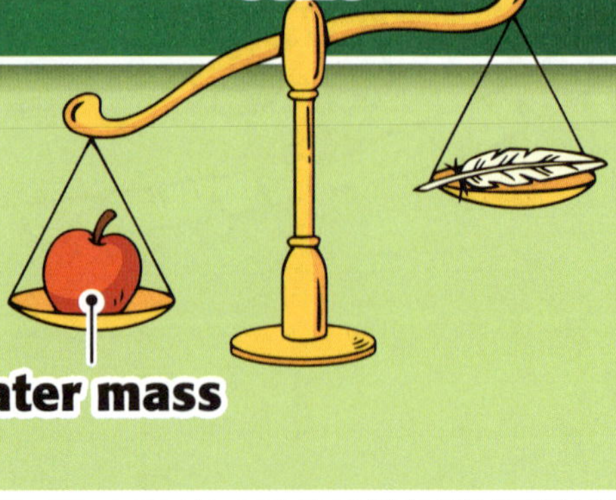

Extension

It is invisible, but it is everywhere. Do you know what it is? It is air! Although we cannot see air, we can certainly feel it. We can feel it as wind and we notice it when it is warm or cold. We can also hear air moving as the wind blows by our ears.

Blowing into Your Hands – *Feel the Air*

Blowing into a Recorder – *Hear the Air*

Think about other ways our senses tell us that air is all around us.

A. Check ✔ the things that show that air takes up space.

Air Takes up Space

B. Check ✔ the things that are moved by air.

Air Makes Things Move

C. Read what the child says. Then color and circle the correct answers.

1. Color the balloon that has more air in it.
2. Circle the heavier balloon.

Air Has Mass

The balloon that has more air in it is heavier. This shows that air **has / does not have** mass.

D. **Draw a line to match each picture with the correct property of air.**

A ball weighs more when it is inflated than when it is deflated.

Properties of Air

- Air takes up space.
- Air makes things move.
- Air has mass.

2 Air in the Environment

Air makes up the atmosphere, which is the layer of gases that surrounds Earth. In this unit, you will recognize air and the ways we can feel its existence.

After completing this unit, you will

- be able to identify things that show that air exists.
- understand that living things need air.
- know that the temperature of air can be measured.

Vocabulary

atmosphere: layer of air surrounding Earth

environment: natural world around us

Extension

We often hear that morning air is fresh, but do you know why? One reason is that with less traffic early in the morning, there is less smoke and fewer pollutants from cars. Secondly, when plants make food, they absorb sunlight and carbon dioxide (a gas that we breathe out as waste) and release oxygen (a gas we breathe in that our body needs). Take a walk early in the morning and you will feel refreshed and energized!

A. Check ✔ the things that show air exists.

B. Read the poem. Then list the living things mentioned in the poem and answer the questions.

Who Needs Air?

A fish in water
A tall pine tree
A potato vine
A buzzing bee

A big blue whale
A tiny bug
A bunny and its carrots
A slimy slug

We're all living but
There's more we share
To stay alive
We all need air.

1. Living things like

   ______________, ______________,
   ______________, ______________,
   ______________, ______________,
   ______________, ______________,
   and ______________ need air.

2. Apart from food, water, and warmth, what do living things need?

   ____

3. Could living things stay alive if there were no air?

   ____

C. Unscramble the words to complete the rhymes.

1. 

This cup is not empty; it's full of air.

It can't be seen, but it's surely ________ .
rtehe

2. 

Wind is merely moving air.

Seen in the trees, felt in your ________ .
iahr

3. 

Smoke and exhaust pollute the air.

It affects us all, so we all should ________ .
erca

D. Fill in the blanks with the correct words. Then check ✔ the correct temperatures.

Fahrenheit thermometer temperature

The 1. ____________ of air describes how hot or cold it is. We measure temperature with a 2. ____________ that tells how hot or cold it is in degrees 3. ____________ or Celcius.

4.

The temperature is low when it is cold.

Ⓐ 23°F (-5°C)

Ⓑ 86°F (30°C)

5.

Ⓐ 23°F (-5°C)

Ⓑ 86°F (30°C)

3 Water and Its Three States

Although water may seem basic, it has its own unique and special properties. In this unit, you will learn about the properties of water and its three states.

After completing this unit, you will

- know the properties of water.
- know the three states that water exists in.

Vocabulary

odorless: having no smell

evaporate: (of a liquid) to turn into a gas

Extension

During cool seasons, we often hear from weather news that a "frost advisory" is in effect. Do you know why this warning is needed? When the temperature falls to a level at which the water in the air freezes, frost will form on surfaces. Frost is harmless for the most part, but it can damage delicate outdoor plants, especially those with soft stems and large leaves. Watering the plants thoroughly and covering them up are some ways to protect them from frost.

A. Check ✔ the properties of water.

Properties of Water

- (A) odorless
- (B) sweet
- (C) yellow
- (D) colorless
- (E) clear
- (F) tasteless
- (G) has mass
- (H) flows when not in a container
- (I) takes up space

B. Label the water in each state "solid," "liquid," or "gas." Then fill in the blanks with the correct words.

States of Water

The water that makes up an ice cube will ______________ into liquid water. That water will ______________ into gas (also called vapor) in the air, or the water will ______________ and become ice again.

C. Complete the diagrams with "heat," "cool," or "freeze."

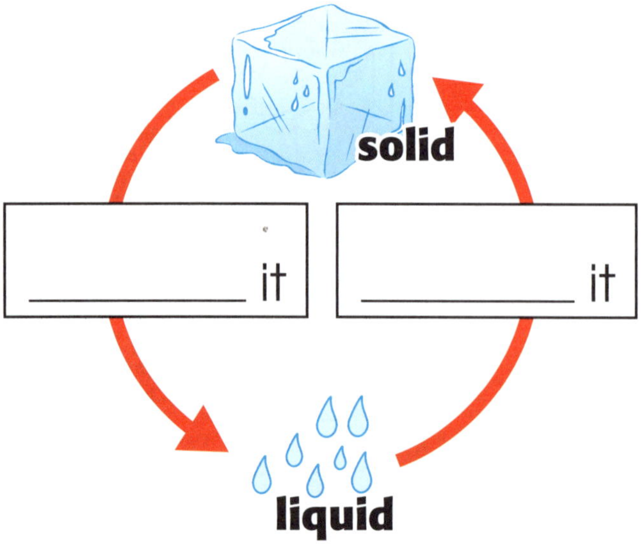

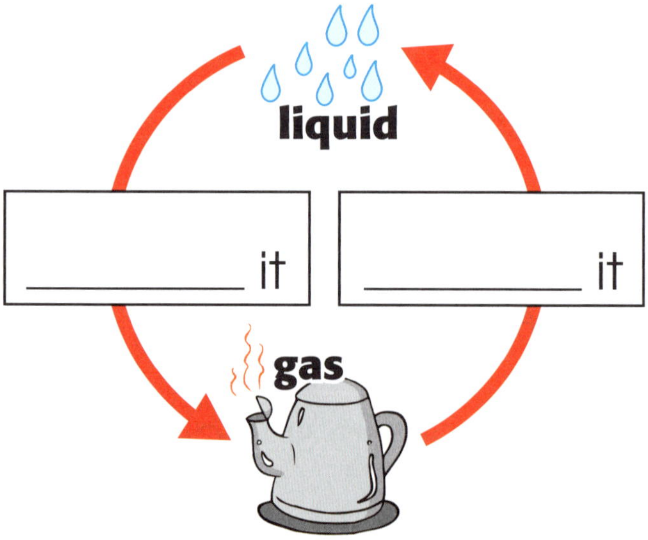

D. Check ✔ the pictures that show the existence of water. Then name the states it is in.

1. 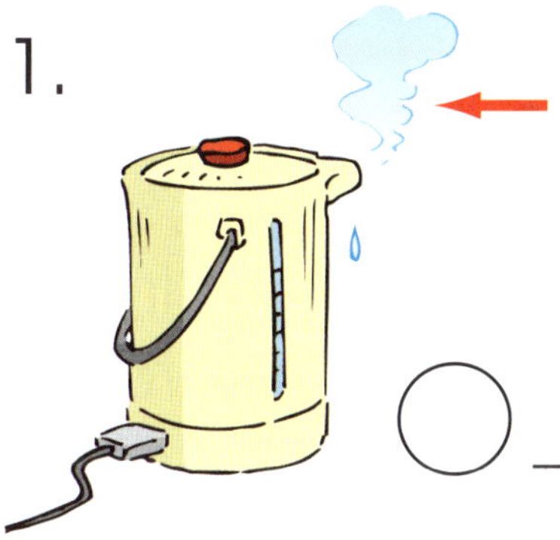

◯ ____________________

2. 

◯ ____________________

3. 

◯ ____________________

4. 

◯ ____________________

E. Circle the correct word for each sentence with the help of the picture. Then answer the question.

1. 

Glaciers / Cashmere can be found in the North Pole.

2. 

The **leaf / rain** gets absorbed into the ground where it falls.

3. *Are the circled answers forms of water? If so, write the state of water for each.*

____

4 Water in the Environment

Water is a big part of our environment. In this unit, you will see that water is in the ground and in the air. You will also learn that it exists as different forms of precipitation.

After completing this unit, you will

- know some forms of moisture in the environment.
- know that the water cycle involves evaporation, condensation, and precipitation.

Vocabulary

evaporation: water changing from liquid to gas

condensation: water changing from gas to liquid

precipitation: water falling from the sky as rain, snow, or hail

Extension

Snowflakes are a solid form of water, like ice cubes. If you look at them very closely, you will see that they have beautiful formations. Did you know that

- *every snowflake has its own unique shape?*
- *no two snowflakes are exactly the same?*
- *most snowflakes have six sides?*

The next time you see fluffy snowflakes drifting down from the sky, don't forget to take a closer look at them.

Different Types of Snowflakes

A. Solve the riddles with the correct words. Then for each form of moisture, write "S" for solid and "L" for liquid.

These are some forms of moisture in our environment. They are either solid or liquid.

hail **snow**
rain **frost**

1. It falls from dark clouds and comes in droplets. ____________ ○

2. It is flaky and no two of its crystals are exactly the same. ____________ ○

3. It is ice that falls from the sky. ____________ ○

4. You may see these ice crystals on surfaces on a winter morning. ____________ ○

B. Draw lines to match the words with the descriptions. Then label the diagram with the words in bold, trace the arrows, and answer the question.

Three Main Stages of the Water Cycle

Evaporation •	• Evaporated water condenses, turning into liquid.
Condensation •	• Water evaporates, becoming a gas.
Precipitation •	• Liquid water becomes heavy and falls as rain, snow, or hail.

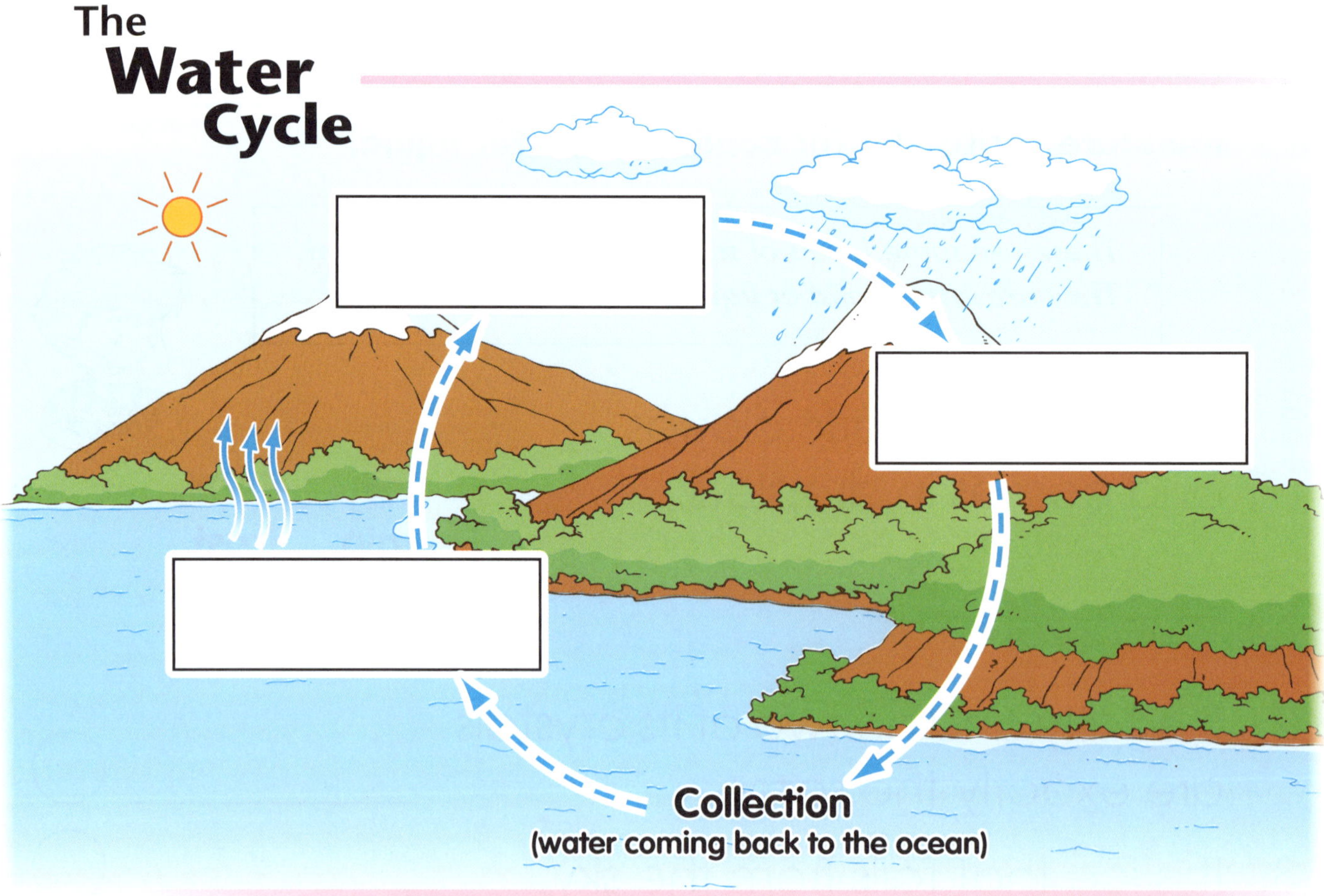

Where does the water cycle get its energy from? ______________

C. Determine whether each description is about "evaporation," "condensation," or "precipitation."

1. 

The steam from a hot shower fogs up a mirror.

____

2. 

The storm can cover a city in white.

____

3. 

The morning dew on the leaves has disappeared by noon.

____

4. 

The towel that was hung up has dried.

____

5. *Droplets of water formed on the outer wall of my cup of cold drink.*

____

5 Water Sources and Uses

We have many uses for water and different ways of getting water. In this unit, you will learn about water sources and how we get water to our homes for use.

After completing this unit, you will

- know where we get our water.
- understand how water gets to our homes.
- learn how we use water.

Vocabulary

fresh water: not salt water; usually from rivers, lakes, rain, or underground

filter: remove impurities

Sources of Fresh Water

Extension

As you know, water is essential to us. We can live for a few weeks without food, but without water, we can only survive for a few days. So we must keep ourselves hydrated to stay healthy. But did you know that there are different types of drinking water?

tap water: *water from our faucets*

glacier water: *water sourced from glaciers*

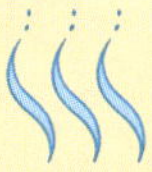

distilled water: *condensed liquid water collected from the steam formed from boiled water*

A. Label the pictures with the correct words. Then fill in the blank.

lake river well

Where We Get Our Water

1. ____________

2. ____________

3. ____________

These are important sources of 4. ____________ water.
fresh/salt

B. Read the paragraph. Then complete the diagram with the words in bold and answer the questions.

In most cities and towns, water comes from a public water system. Water can be moved from a **lake**, a natural freshwater source, to a human-made **water treatment plant** where it is filtered, cleaned, and treated so that it is safe to drink. It is then moved to homes and businesses through a **water supply system** of pipes and pumps.

1. **How Water Gets to You:**

2. What does a water treatment plant do? Why are its functions important?

____

____

C. **Check ✔ the uses of water.**

How do we use water?

Daily Activity

- ◯ cooking
- ◯ vacuuming
- ◯ bathing
- ◯ drinking
- ◯ mopping
- ◯ writing

Transportation

- ◯ ship
- ◯ car
- ◯ airplane
- ◯ submarine
- ◯ bus
- ◯ speedboat

Appliance

- ◯ air conditioner
- ◯ dishwasher
- ◯ television
- ◯ computer
- ◯ toaster
- ◯ washing machine

Sports

◯ 

- ◯ swimming
- ◯ skiing

Leisure

◯ 

- ◯ reading
- ◯ making pottery

6 Air and Water Pollution

While we need both air and water to live, we often waste or pollute them. In this unit, you will see how human activities pollute air and water, and you will learn about what we can do to help protect the environment.

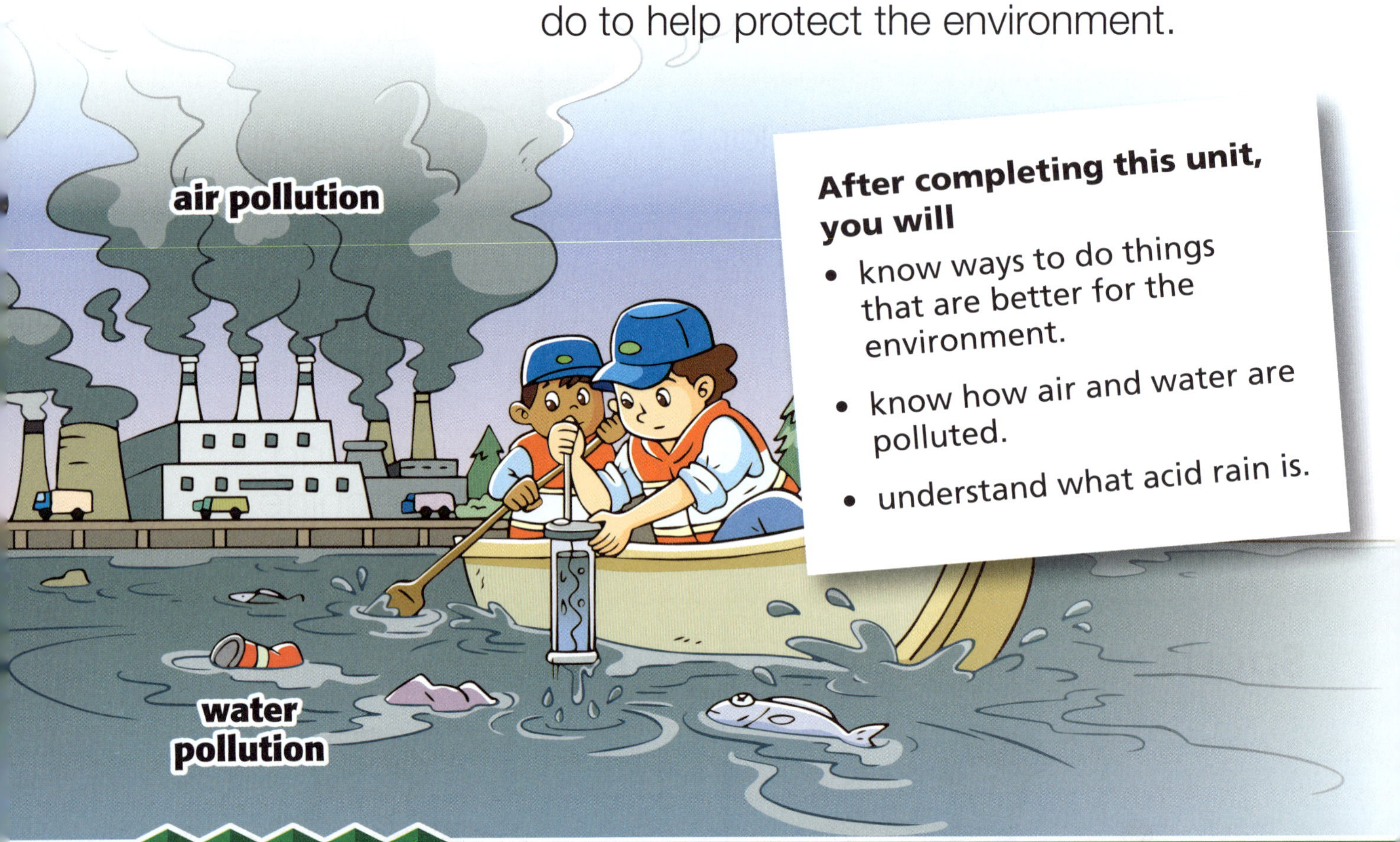

After completing this unit, you will

- know ways to do things that are better for the environment.
- know how air and water are polluted.
- understand what acid rain is.

Vocabulary

pollution: the result of activities that are harmful to the environment

salt water: water from oceans and seas; not suitable for drinking

Extension

It is fresh water, not salt water, that we can drink. But the salt water in oceans and seas makes up most of Earth's water. Almost all fresh water is frozen in glaciers. This is expensive to obtain, so our fresh water is limited. We should make good use of the fresh water we do have and not waste it. Think about some of the things you can do to use water smartly.

A. Check ✔ the way of doing each task that is better for our environment.

1. 

   (A) Run a dishwasher after every meal.

   (B) Run a dishwasher only when it is full.

2. 

   (A) Water the lawn even after it has rained.

   (B) Water the lawn only when needed.

3. 

   (A) Install water-saving toilets.

   (B) Install the most expensive toilets.

4. 

   (A) Turn off the faucet when you brush your teeth.

   (B) Leave the water running until you are done brushing.

B. Fill in the blanks with the correct words. Then circle the correct words for the solutions.

Things That Pollute the Air and Water

farming coal fuel spills
oil car factories

1. 

_______________ often pollute the environment, releasing harmful substances into the air and water.

Solution **Follow / Don't follow** government guidelines to dispose of waste responsibly.

2. 

_______________ often involves pesticides to keep bugs away and fertilizers to make crops grow quickly, but both substances get into the water and pollute it.

Solution **Use / Don't use** safe and organic growing methods whenever possible.

3. 

We burn ________________ and ________________ to make electricity, but this causes air and water pollution.

Solution Use clean energy such as wind and **water / fossil fuels** to make electricity.

4. 

Driving a ________________ can cause air pollution, and ________________ from vehicles, including ships, cause water pollution.

Solution Instead of driving, walk, bike, or take **public transit / a cab** whenever possible.

C. Read about acid rain. Then answer the questions.

When polluted air mixes with water vapor, acid rain is formed. Acid rain contains acidic components that can harm living things, including plants and fish.

1. How is acid rain formed?

____

____

2. What can acid rain harm?

____

WATER IN THE AIR

understanding that there is water in the air

A weather forecast not only tells us the highest and lowest temperatures during the day, it also tells us about the humidity. Do you know what humidity is? Humidity is the amount of water that is in the air. We normally cannot see water in the air but it is everywhere. Try this experiment to make this surrounding water visible.

What you need:

a cup

water

an ice cube tray

food coloring

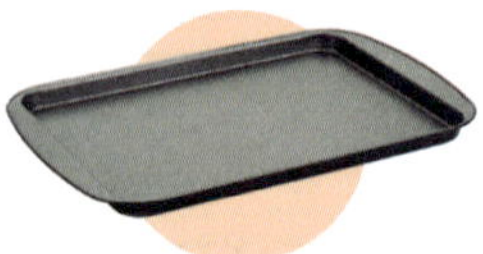

a baking sheet

What to do:

1. Fill the cup with water and add a few drops of the food coloring.

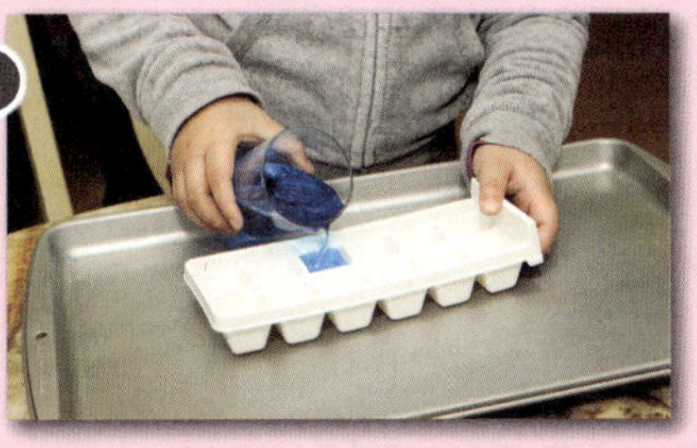

2. Pour the cup of water into the ice cube tray. Freeze it for 2 hours.

3. Put the ice cubes into the cup.

4. Leave the cup on the dry baking sheet for 20 minutes. Then observe.

STEM Note

If there is a lot of water vapor in the air, the humidity will be high. High humidity makes environment feel warmer because the water vapor in the air makes it more difficult for sweat to evaporate from our skin.

Difficulty: ●○○○○

Time needed: 3 hours

In this experiment, you will learn that there is water in the air.

WHAT *just* happened?

In this experiment, you should have noticed that clear water droplets formed outside the cup and there might even be a puddle under the cup. Since this water was colorless, it could not have come from the water inside the cup. So where did this water come from?

This water came from the water vapor in the air around the cup. The cold cup cooled down the water vapor in the air around it, leading to a process called condensation. As the water vapor condensed, it could no longer stay as a gas but changed into tiny water droplets and clung to the outside of the cup. As more and more water vapor condensed on the cup's outer surface, the droplets became bigger and eventually dripped down to form a puddle on the baking sheet.

In nature, the formation of dewdrops on leaves is an example of condensation.

STEM INQUIRY

- Name the states of matter you observed in this experiment.
- What is an example of condensation in the water cycle in nature?
- How do you change water back into water vapor?

- Dehumidifiers are machines that remove water from the air. With the help of an adult, research how these machines work.
- Humidity is the measure of the amount of water in the air. Use a weather website to find out the humidity level in your city with the help of an adult.

- In this experiment, water droplets collected on the outside of the cup. Can you design a cup that prevents or minimizes condensation on the outside?

Fun to know

Water in Our Bodies

So how much water is inside us? There is actually quite a lot! In fact, about three fifths of our body is water. This is because our body relies on water for a lot of essential functions, such as producing saliva for eating, flushing out waste, sweating to stay cool, and much more.

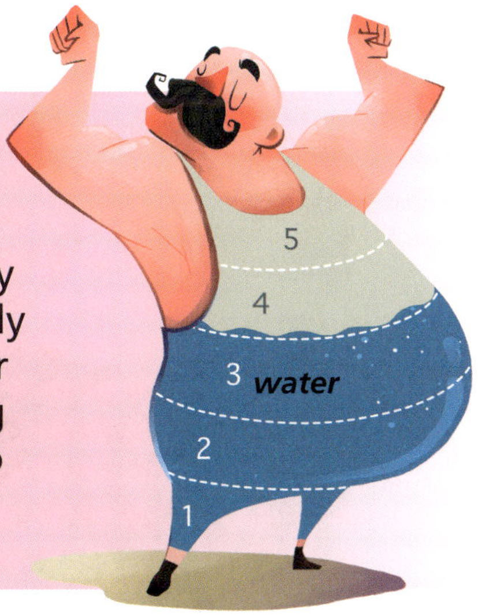

A RAIN JAR

understanding evaporation and condensation

We all enjoy sunny days when we get to play outside and have a good time. But every once in a while, a rainy day shows up and we have to stay indoors. Have you ever wondered where rain comes from and how it forms?

What you need:

a zipper bag

a jar

a plate

water

blue food coloring

Difficulty:
●●○○○

Time needed:
2 days

In this experiment, you will learn how rain forms by creating your own rain.

What to do:

1. Fill the zipper bag with some water. Put it in the freezer and let it freeze overnight.
2. Ask an adult to fill half of the jar with hot tap water. Add a few drops of the blue food coloring.
3. Leave the jar close to the window where it gets lots of sunlight. Place the plate over the jar to cover it.
4. Put the zipper bag with the ice on the plate.
5. Observe the jar after an hour. It will take some time before you can see rain in the jar.

STEM Note

Water freezes at 32°F (0°C).

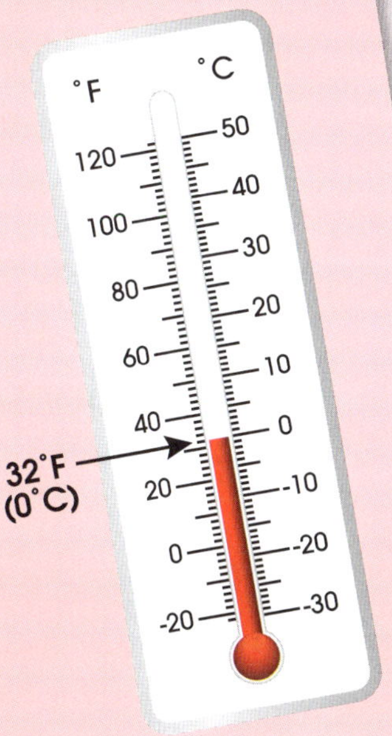

WHAT *just* happened?

You should have seen droplets of water dripping inside the jar. These water droplets are your "rain." At the beginning of the experiment, since the water was hot, it began to evaporate into water vapor. As the water vapor rose, it came into contact with the cold plate which caused the vapor to cool and condense into tiny water droplets. As more and more water droplets gathered, they became too heavy and began dripping down inside the jar like rain falling from clouds.

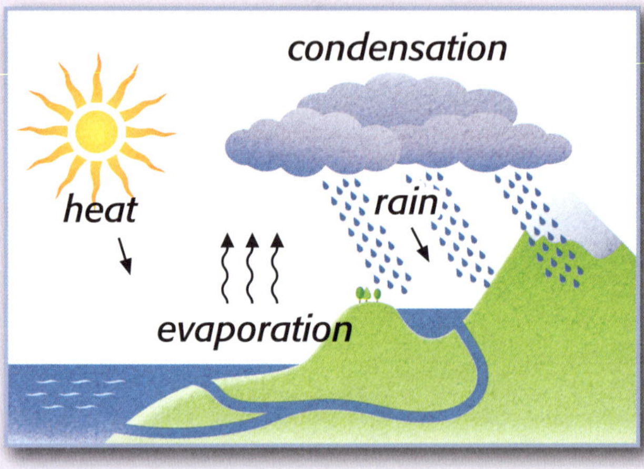

In nature, rain is formed in a similar way. Water from oceans and rivers is heated by the sun, causing it to evaporate into water vapor and rise. As it cools in the sky, the water vapor condenses into water droplets that form rain clouds. When the weight of these rain clouds becomes too heavy, the condensed water droplets fall back to earth as rain.

STEM INQUIRY

- What is the energy source for the water cycle?
- What would happen to the water cycle if we did not have the sun?
- How does the temperature of water influence how quickly it evaporates?

- A rain gauge is a tool used to measure the amount of rainfall. Build a rain gauge using materials found around your home.

- Track the amount of rain received where you live during a month. Make a graph showing the data you have collected.

Fun to know

Snowy Winter

During the cold winter, water droplets fall back down as snow instead of rain. The way snow is formed is similar to rain; water still gets heated and evaporates before cooling again and condensing into clouds. But instead of water droplets combining, the water vapor freezes together to form ice crystals. And once these ice crystals become too heavy, they fall back down as snowflakes!

SALTY SEAWATER

understanding why seawater is salty

Water is everywhere! It is found in oceans, rivers, glaciers, and even underground. It can be hot or cold, or fresh or salty, depending on where you find it. The water in lakes and rivers is usually fresh but the water in seas and oceans is salty. So why is seawater salty?

What you need:

- flour
- salt
- oil
- water
- green food coloring
- a baking sheet
- a craft knife

CAUTION!
Ask an adult to help you use the craft knife.

What to do:

1. Follow the instructions below to make your own dough.
   - Mix 2 cups of flour, 1 cup of salt, and 2 tablespoons of oil.
   - Slowly add 2 cups of warm water and a few drops of the green food coloring to the mixture while stirring. If the dough gets too sticky, add more flour.
2. On the dry baking sheet, make a mountain out of the dough.
3. Make a few rivers on the mountain with the craft knife.
4. Sprinkle 8 teaspoons of salt onto the mountain.
5. Pour 1 cup of water slowly over the mountain.
6. Leave the model for 5 minutes and taste the water collected on the baking sheet.
7. Repeat Steps 5 and 6 twice.
8. Did you notice the water was getting saltier?

Difficulty:
●●●●○

Time needed:
1 hour

In this experiment, you will simulate the journey of rainwater and find out where it goes.

WHAT *just* happened?

The water that you tasted should have got saltier and saltier. The water you poured over the mountain in Step 5 represented rainfall and the water collected on the baking sheet represented seawater.

In nature, when rainwater falls, it lands on different surfaces like mountains, rocks, and soil. The rainwater from all over the land flows into rivers and streams, eventually reaching the ocean. Along its journey, the water picks up minerals, including salt, and carries them to the ocean. Meanwhile, the sun's heat causes more and more water to evaporate, leaving the salt behind over time.

The cycle repeats again and again as more rain falls, dissolves minerals, and reaches the ocean. This is why seawater is salty and why the water on the baking sheet became saltier as more salt on the mountain ran down with the water you poured.

water in a river with dissolved minerals flowing into the ocean

STEM INQUIRY

- How did the rivers created on the dough mountain affect the distribution and movement of water in the experiment?
- Why was the water you tasted salty?
- If the model is left overnight, do you think the water will be even saltier? Why?

- Salt is a mineral. With the help of an adult, do some research to find out what a mineral is. Can you name a few common minerals?
- Desalination is the process of removing salt from seawater. In what sectors is desalination used? Why is desalination useful in these sectors? Research online with the help of an adult to find out.

- How do the ingredients of the dough, including flour, salt, oil, and water, impact the dough's characteristics such as how it feels, how easy it is to shape, and how strong it is?

Fun to know

Salt-free Lakes and Rivers

Have you ever wondered why the water in oceans is salty while the water in lakes and rivers is not? This is because the water in lakes and rivers is constantly on the move. As water from mountains brings minerals into these bodies of water, their channels and pathways carry them away toward the ocean. This prevents minerals from building up in lakes and rivers and keeps them from becoming salty.

RISING AIR

understanding that hot air rises

Have you ever seen a hot-air balloon floating in the sky? Without wings or a powerful engine, how can the hot-air balloon, carrying a basket full of people, fly freely from place to place? What makes this possible?

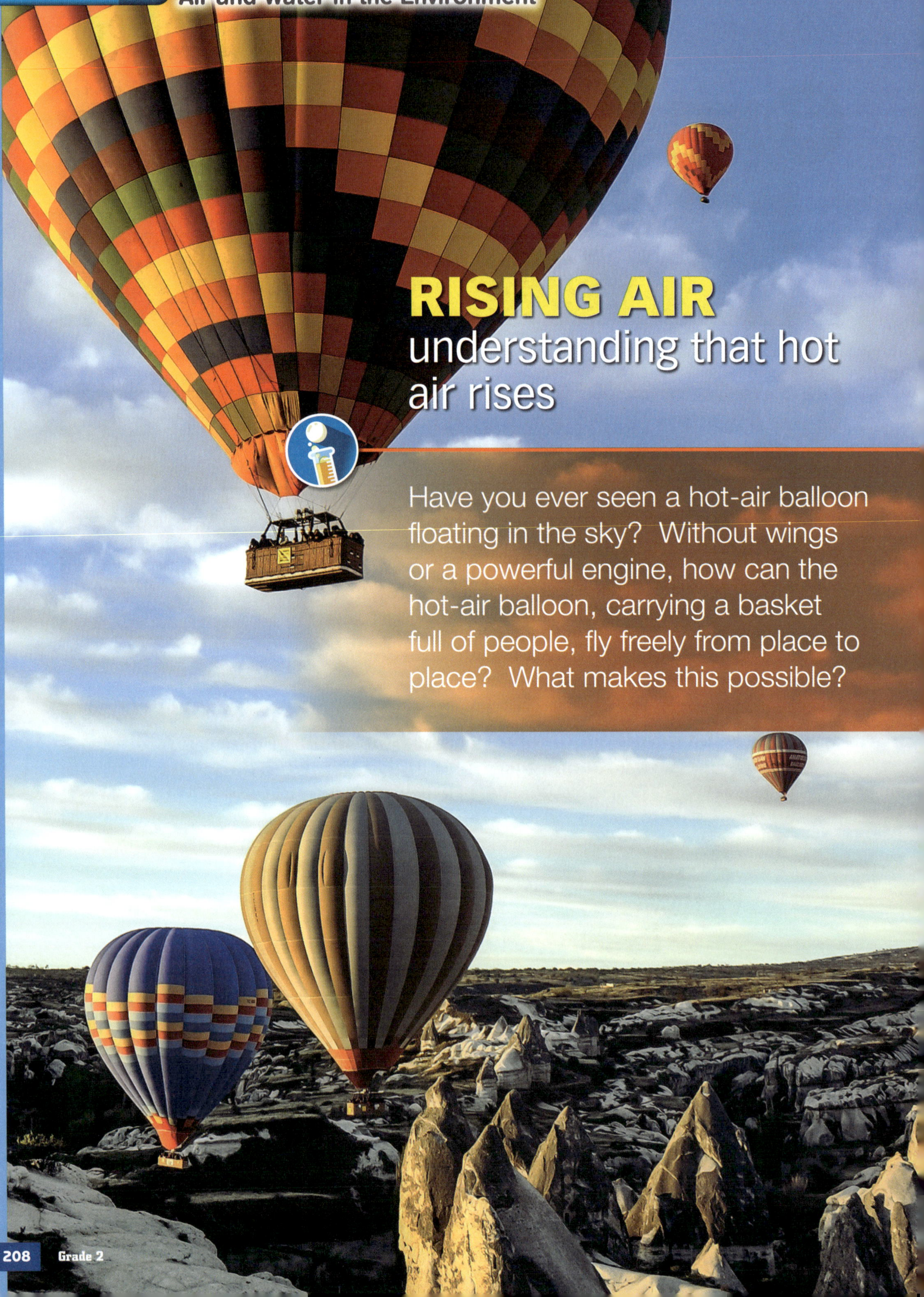

CAUTION!
Have an adult do Steps 4 to 6 for you.

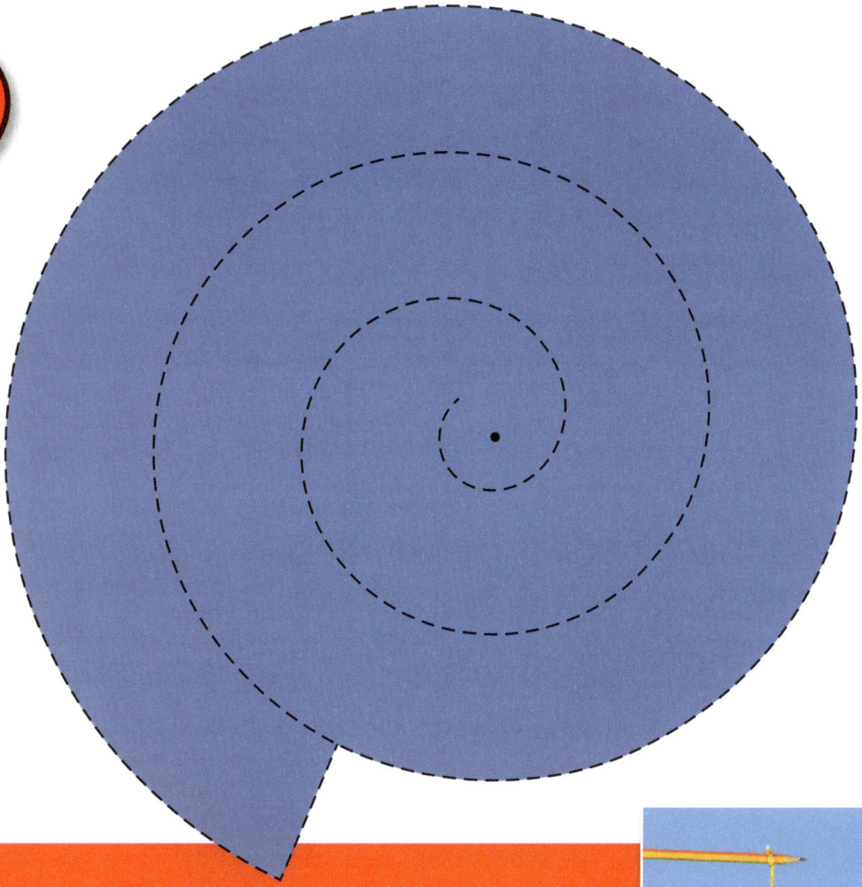

What you need:

scissors

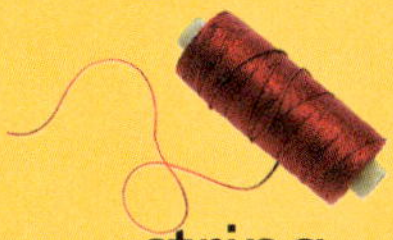
string

a glass jar

a pencil

a candle

a lighter

paper

Difficulty: ●●●●○

Time needed: 30 minutes

In this experiment, you will see that heat causes air to rise.

What to do:

1. Trace the paper spiral above onto a piece of paper.
2. Cut along the dotted line to make a paper spiral. Then poke a hole at the dot for the string.
3. Cut the string into 8″ (about 20 cm). Connect the spiral and the pencil with the string.
4. Place the candle inside the jar and light it.
5. Lift the spiral up using the pencil and wait until it stays still.
6. Hold the spiral over the jar opening. Then observe. Remember to blow out the candle after the experiment.

WHAT *just* happened?

In this experiment, you should have seen that the spiral started spinning above the flame. This is because the air inside the jar was heated up, became less dense, and rose. As the hot air moved past the spiral, it caused the spiral to spin.

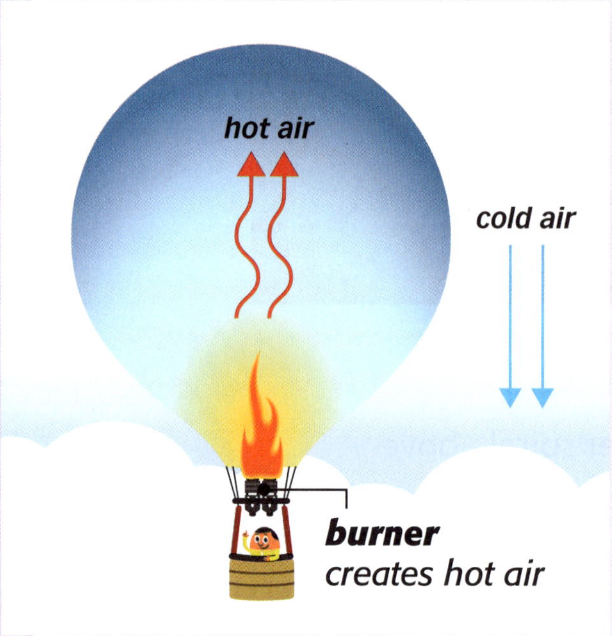

Hot-air balloons make use of this property of hot air to fly in the sky. A burner in the balloon heats up the air inside the balloon, causing it to rise and lift the balloon.

STEM INQUIRY

- How does the distance between the spiral and the flame affect the spinning motion of the spiral?
- Ask an adult to light the candle again and repeat Steps 5 and 6. Then, while holding the spiral over the jar opening, have the adult carefully cover the jar with a lid to put out the flame. What happened when the flame was put out? Did the spinning motion of the spiral stop immediately or gradually?

- Can other heat sources, instead of a candle, be used for the experiment? How does the selection of the heat source affect the way the spiral behaves?
- Why is it important to use a glass jar to contain the candle? Why should a plastic jar not be used in the experiment?

- Find how long the spiral is using a piece of string to trace the spiral's path and then measuring the string's length with a ruler. Can you think of another method to measure the length of the spiral?

Fun to know

Sky Lanterns

The earliest form of hot-air balloons was called sky lanterns. They were not used to carry passengers but instead used for signaling during wars. They were made of paper and, like today's hot-air balloons, had an opening at the bottom where the flame was placed. They are still in use today but not for war. Instead, they are used for fun and at festivals.

THE FORCE OF AIR

understanding how air pressure is at work

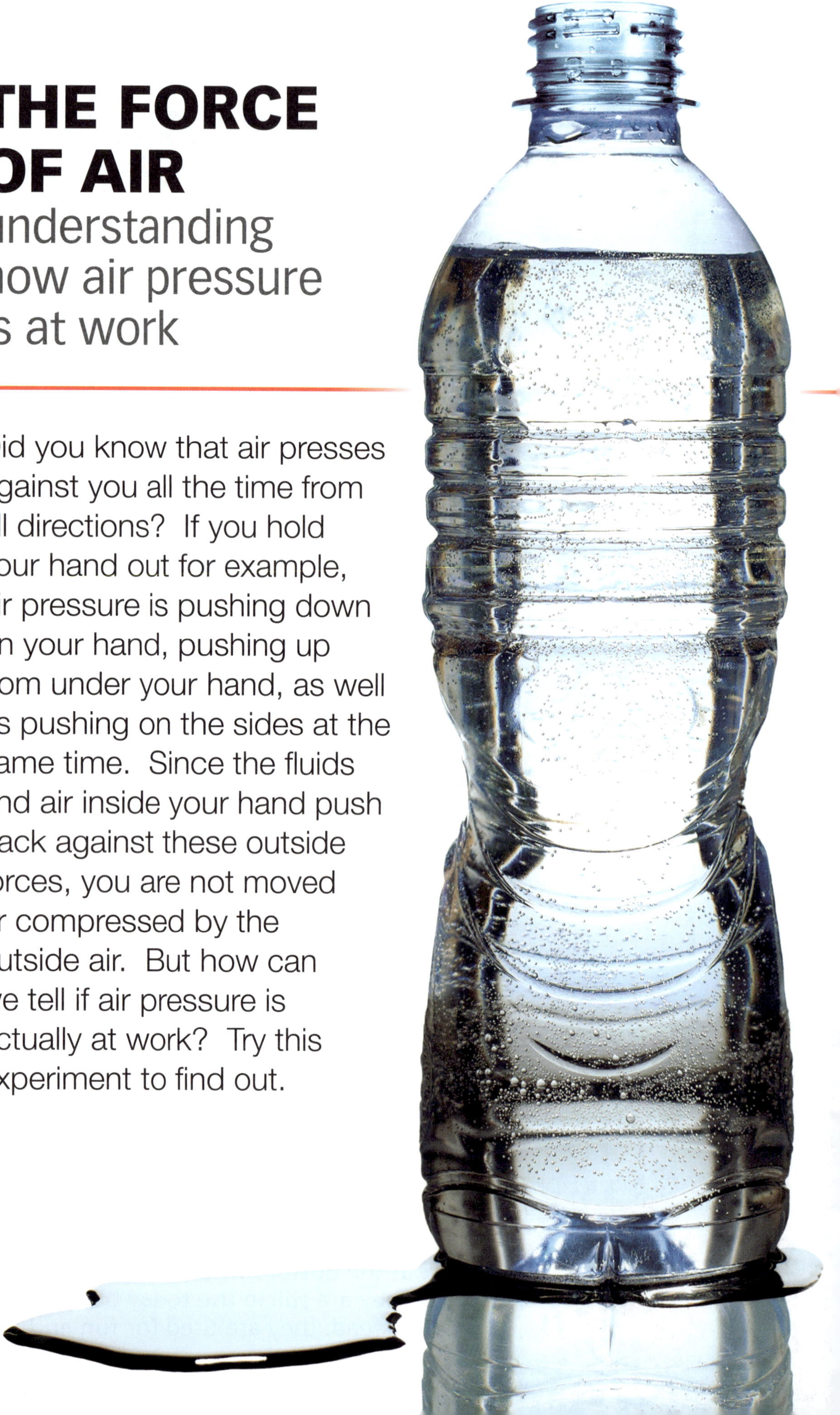

Did you know that air presses against you all the time from all directions? If you hold your hand out for example, air pressure is pushing down on your hand, pushing up from under your hand, as well as pushing on the sides at the same time. Since the fluids and air inside your hand push back against these outside forces, you are not moved or compressed by the outside air. But how can we tell if air pressure is actually at work? Try this experiment to find out.

What you need:

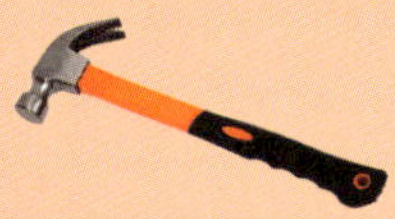

a hammer

a plastic water bottle with a cap

a nail

water

tape

Difficulty:
●●●○○

Time needed:
10 minutes

In this experiment, you will learn about the force of air and see it in action.

What to do:

1. Ask an adult to help you make a small hole in the bottom of the water bottle with the hammer and the nail.
2. Cover the hole with the tape and fill the bottle with water.
3. Screw the cap onto the bottle and hold it over a sink.
4. Gently pull the tape off the bottom of the bottle and observe. Did any water come out?
5. Unscrew the cap and observe. Did any water come out?
6. Try screwing and unscrewing the cap a few times. What did you see?

WHAT *just* happened?

Were you surprised that no water came out from the hole when the cap was on the bottle? This is because air pressure was at work.

When the cap was on the bottle, the water tried to flow out due to the pull of gravity. However, it was unable to do so because there was nothing to take up the space that was originally filled by the water if the water were to flow out. Additionally, air below the hole pushed up against the pull of gravity on the water. Because these two forces were in balance, the water stayed in the bottle.

When the cap was unscrewed, air entered the bottle and pushed down on the water. The pull of gravity, together with the force of the air entering the bottle, was enough to move the water out of the bottle.

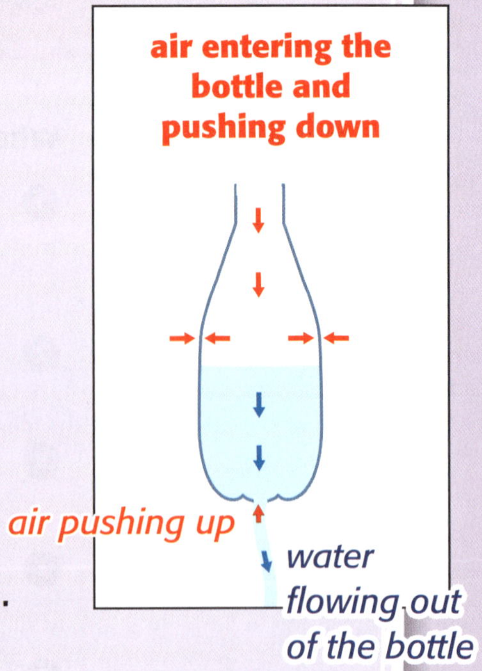

When you screwed and unscrewed the cap, you actually controlled the water flow using air.

STEM INQUIRY

- Do you think the size of the hole makes a difference to the result?
- Does it matter where the hole is made on the bottle?
- What simple machines can you identify in this experiment?

- Meteorologists often mention air pressure. How does air pressure affect weather? With the help of an adult, do some research online to find out.

- Suction cups are tools that use air pressure to stick to surfaces. What are some examples of suction cups being used in your everyday life?

Fun to know

Suction Cups

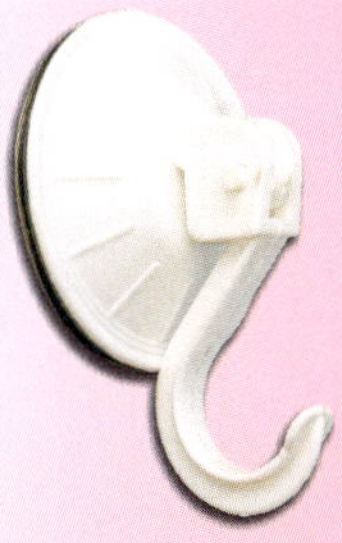

Suction cups are amazing. Without glue, tape, or any sort of adhesive, they are able to stick to surfaces firmly. This is because of air pressure. Suction cups are made of elastic and flexible material. When a suction cup is pressed against a flat surface, the air between the suction cup and the surface is squeezed out, creating a pocket with less air. Since the amount of air outside the suction cup is greater compared to the air inside, it pushes the suction cup against the surface, holding it firmly in place.

Answers

Answers

Section 1

1 Animals – Parts of the Body

A.

B. 1. A
D
2. C
D
3. A
B
D
4. A
D
5. a tail
6-7. (Suggested answers)
6. frog
7. crab

C. 1. shell
2. tail
3. ears
4. feet

D.

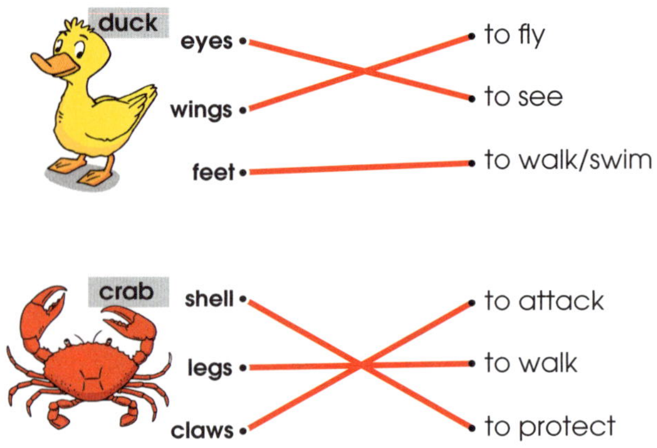

E. 1a. F
b. T
c. F
d. T
e. T
2.

2 Animal Characteristics

A. 1. deer
   2. grasshopper

B. 1. predator
   2. prey
   3.

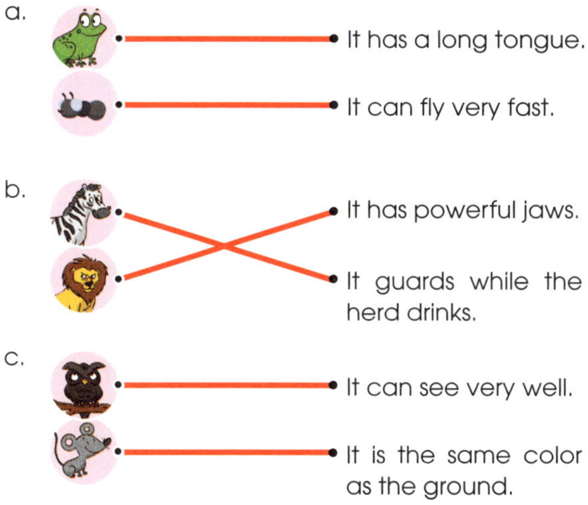

C. (Individual examples)
   1. mammal
   2. fish
   3. reptile
   4. bird
   5. amphibian

D. 1. C
   2. A
   3. A
   4. A ; D ; E

3 Animals – Growth and Changes

A. 1. 3 ; 1 ; 2
   2. 2 ; 1 ; 3
   3. 2 ; 3 ; 1

B. 1. bear ; cub
   2. zebra ; foal
   3. ladybug ; nymph
   4. seal ; pup
   5. frog ; tadpole

C. (Suggested answers)
   1. lion and panda
   2. baby elephant

D. 1. butterfly
   2. duck
   3. mouse
   4. frog

E. 1a. F
   b. T
   c. F
   d. T
   2. B
   3. C
   4. C
   5. C

4 Life Cycles of Animals

A.

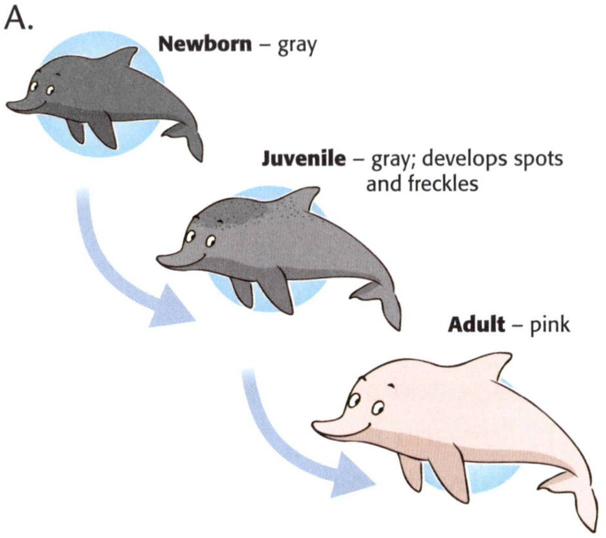

B. 1. B
   2. C
   3. A

C. 1. egg
   2. caterpillar
   3. chrysalis
   4. butterfly

D. 1. They hatch from their eggs on land.
   2. They hatch after about 50 days.
   3. They rush to the water from the beach and begin swimming.
   4. (Suggested answer)
   Chickens and fish hatch from eggs.
   5. A

5 Animal Adaptations

A.

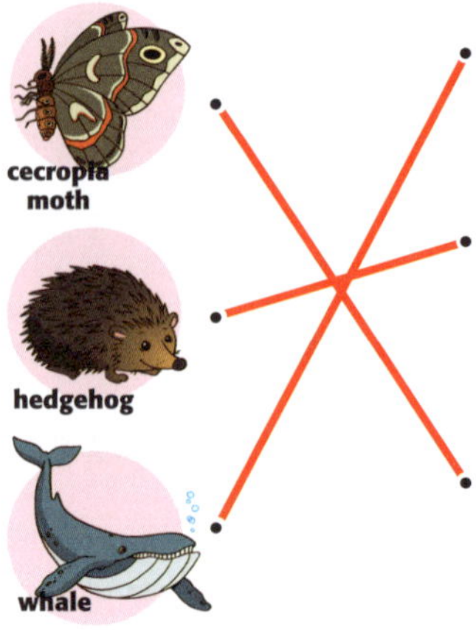

- Its flippers allow it to steer, turn, and balance.
- It is covered with needlelike spines that can ward off predators.
- Its wings have the pattern of a snake. This is believed to scare predators away.

B. 1. color
   2. color ; pattern

C. cold ; sleep ; hibernation ; little

D. place ; south ; winter
monarch butterfly ; salmon ; seabird

E. 1. migrates
2. hibernates
3. camouflages

F. 1. Mimicry enables an animal to take on the appearance of other animals, while camouflage allows an animal to blend into its surroundings.
2. Mimicry allows an animal to look like an animal that is more dangerous or poisonous, which scares away potential predators.
3. C
4. B

6 Human and Animal Interactions

A. 1. Sheep
2. Dogs
3. Bees
4. Cows

B. 1. diseases
2. crops
3. allergic
4. dangerous
5. threat

C. 1. mosquito ; ant ; No
2. fox ; beaver ; No
3. dog ; cat ; Yes
4. moose ; bear ; Yes
5. deer ; elephant ; sheep ; No

D.1a. T
b. F
c. T
2. (Suggested answer)
Dogs are loving, playful, and obedient.
3.

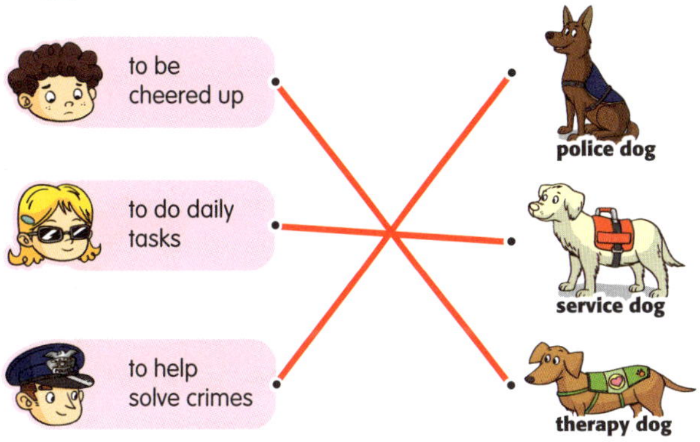

Section 2

1 Position

A. 1. A, D
   B, C
2. near

B. 1. above
2. behind
3. under
4. on
5. in
6. in front of
7. beside

C. 1.

up

2.

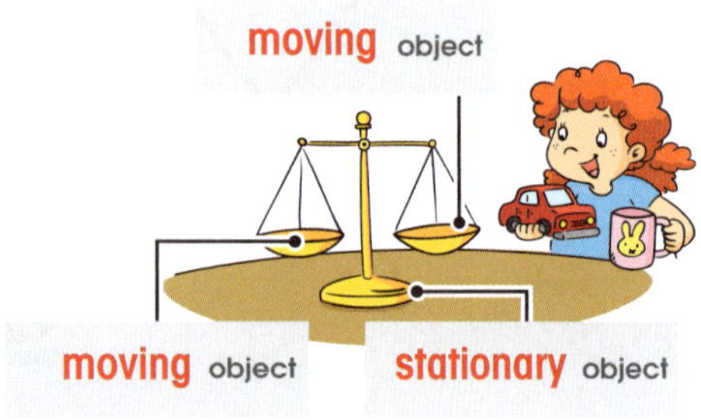

down ; up

D. 1. B
2. A
3.

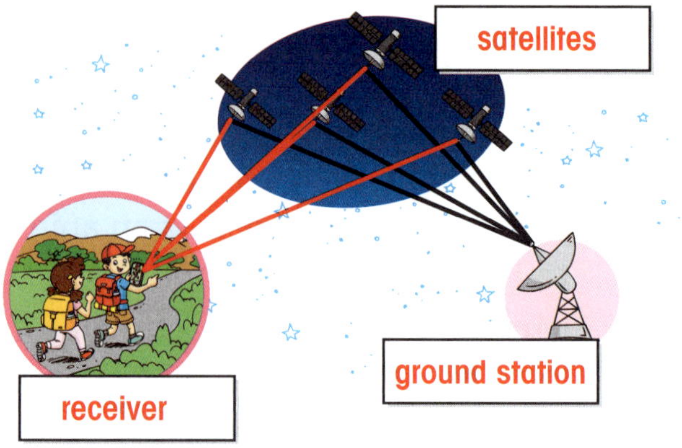

2 Movement

A. 1. Push
2. Pull
3. Push
4. Push
5. Pull

B. A: Jump
B: Climb
C: Slide
D: Spin
E: Bounce
F: Swing

C. 1. spinning
2. bouncing
3. vibrating
4. swinging
5. sliding
6. rolling
7. turning

D. 1. B ; C ; A
2. You can bounce, spin, and roll a basketball.
3. The movements that are involved are spinning and jumping.
4. (Individual drawing and writing)

3 Simple Machines (1)

A. B ; inclined plane
A ; wedge
C ; lever

B.

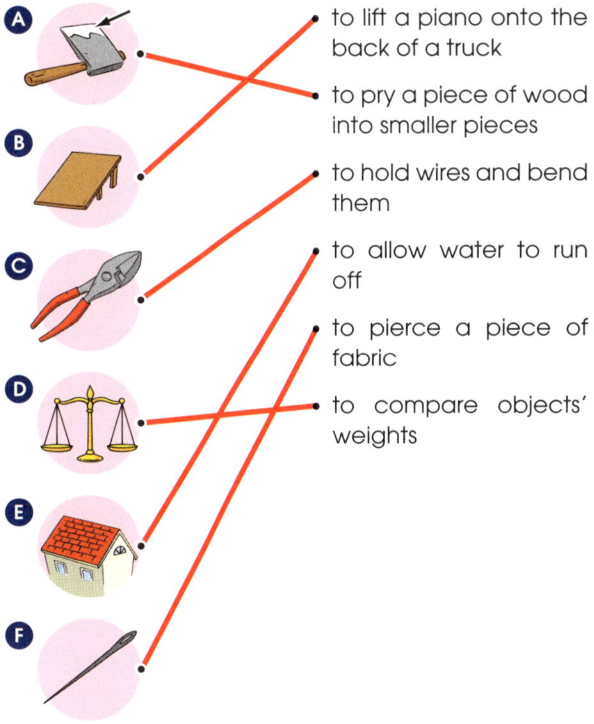

Lever: C ; D
Inclined Plane: B ; E
Wedge: A ; F

C. (Individual examples)
A: wedge
B: lever
C: inclined plane
D: inclined plane
E: wedge
F: lever

D. 1. B ; D ; E

2. (Suggested answer)
The examples are slides in parks and ski hills in nature.

3. A ramp, which is an inclined plane, helps people access buildings without using stairs.

4. (Color the longer ramp.)

4 Simple Machines (2)

A.

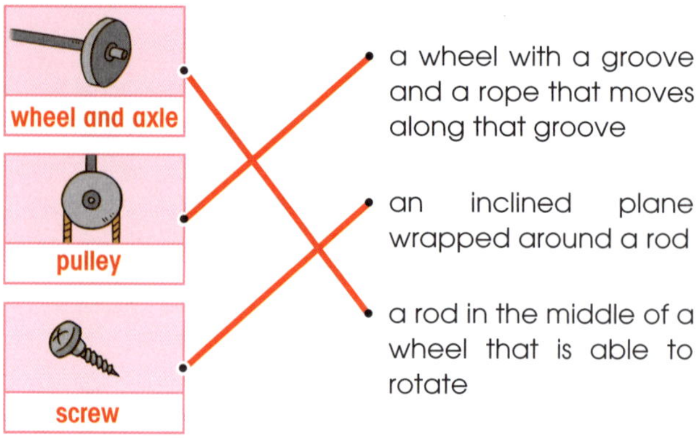

B.

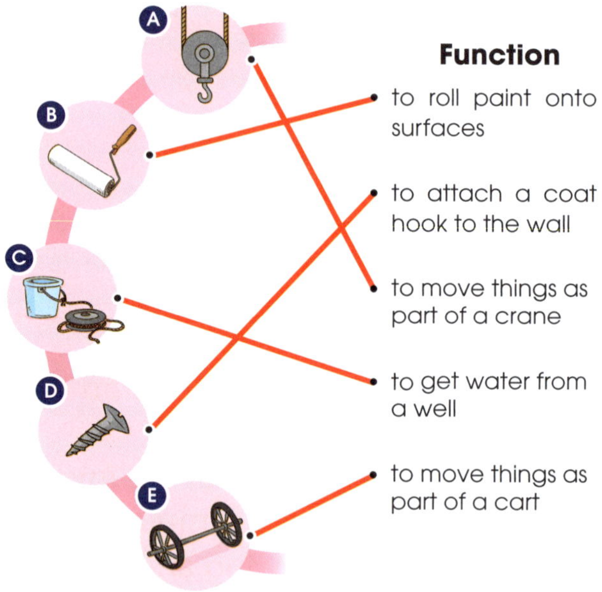

Pulley: A, C
Wheel and Axle: B, E
Screw: D

C. (Individual examples)
1. pulley
2. screw
3. wheel and axle
4. wheel and axle
5. screw
6. pulley

D. 1.

2. (Suggested examples)

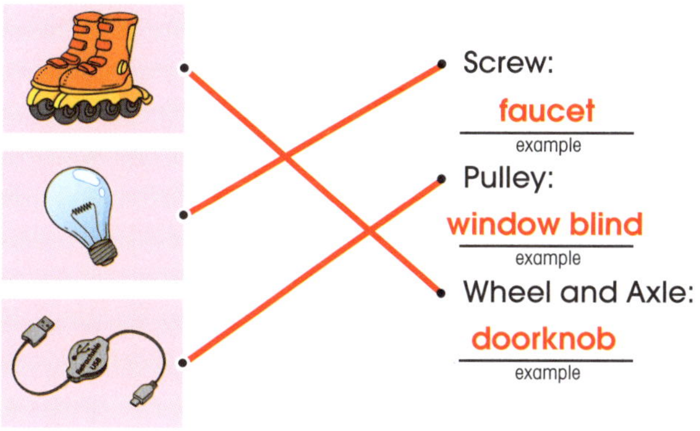

5 Machines in Action

A. 1. lever ; wedge
2. lever ; wheel and axle

B.

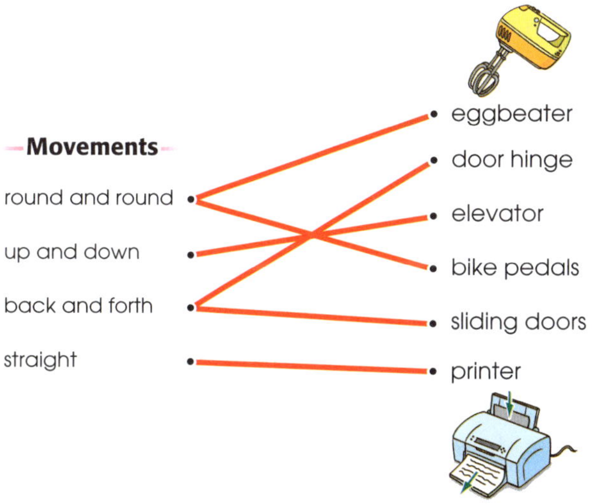

C. (Suggested examples)
Round and Round: clock hands
Up and Down: window blinds
Back and Forth: pendulum
Straight: slides

D. (Suggested examples)
1. E ; spoon
2. B ; nail
3. A ; wheelbarrow
4. D ; swing
5. F ; tweezers
6. C ; plane

E. 1. (Trace lines as indicated.)
back and forth ; round and round
2. The floor of the carousel moves round and round and the horses move up and down.

6 Uses of Simple Machines

A. 1. cutting
   2. raises
   3. moves
   4. down
   5. holds
   6. up and down

B. 1. inclined plane
   A
   longer
   2. wedge
   B
   sharper

C. safely
   clean
   after
   Tie up
   Remove
   eyes

D. 1. He was an American engineer and cartoonist. He is known for creating Rube Goldberg machines.
   2. They are inventions that did simple jobs in complicated ways.
   3. 5
   2
   4
   7
   6
   3

Section 3

1 Liquids

A. From Nature: B, C, E
   Human-made: A, D, F

B. 1. A ; C ; E ; I ; J
   2. can ; takes ; can

C. chocolate milk: opaque ; runny
   ketchup: opaque
   cooking oil: clear ; runny ; greasy
   1. cooking oil
   2. ketchup
   3. chocolate milk

2 Solids

A. Human-made: A ; B ; D
From Nature: C ; E ; F

B. 1-4. (Suggested answers)
1. straw
ice
2. glass bowl
pebbles
3. watering can
flower
4. paintbrush
paint can

B ; C

C. 1. opaque
soft
light
2. granular
smooth
opaque
3. rough
heavy
hard
4. smooth
clear
hard
5. (Individual examples)

3 Liquids and Solids (1)

A.

B. 1. solid
A ; C ; F ; H
2. liquid
B ; D ; E ; G

C. 1. Paint: sticky ; opaque ; thick
Sponge: soft ; light
Rice: hard ; granular
2. (Individual examples)

Answers

4 Liquids and Solids (2)

A. 1. buoyant
   2. repels
   3. absorbs
   4. dissolves

B. (Individual examples)
   Buoyant: A, B, F
   Not Buoyant: C, D, E

C. 1. absorbs
   2. repels
   3. absorbs
   4. repels
   5. absorbs

D. blocks and marbles: do not mix
   oil and water: do not mix
   lemon juice and water: mix
   sand in water: sinks
   cork in water: floats
   sock in water: absorbs
   sugar in water: dissolves

5 Changes of State

A. 1a. liquid
   b. solid
   2. solid
   3. liquid
   4. solid

B. 1. solid ; liquid
   melts ; ✔
   2. solid ; solid
   broken ; ✘
   3. liquid ; solid
   cooled ; ✔
   4. liquid ; liquid
   spilled ; ✘

C. 1. solid
   freezes ; ice
   2. liquid
   melts ; water

D. 1. freezes
   liquid
   solid
   2. melts
   solid
   liquid

6 Safety with Liquids and Solids

A. spills
warnings
mix
containers
children

B. 1. explosive ; heated
2. flammable ; fire
3. corrosive ; burn
4. poisonous ; swallowed
5.

6.

C. (Suggested answers)
1. No, it will no longer be safe to skate because the ice will become too thin to support the skater.
2. No, it will no longer be safe to drive because snow will make it more difficult to see and the roads will become very slippery.

Section 4

1 What Is Air?

A. A ; C ; E

B.

C. 1. (Color the larger balloon.)
2. (Circle the larger balloon.)
has

D.

2 Air in the Environment

A.

B. 1. fish ; pine trees ; potato vines ; bees ; blue whales ; bugs ; bunnies ; carrots ; slugs
   2. air
   3. no

C. 1. there
   2. hair
   3. care

D. 1. temperature
   2. thermometer
   3. Fahrenheit
   4. 23°F (-5°C)
   5. 86°F (30°C)

3 Water and Its Three States

A. A ; D ; E ; F ; G ; H ; I

B.

melt ; evaporate ; freeze

C.

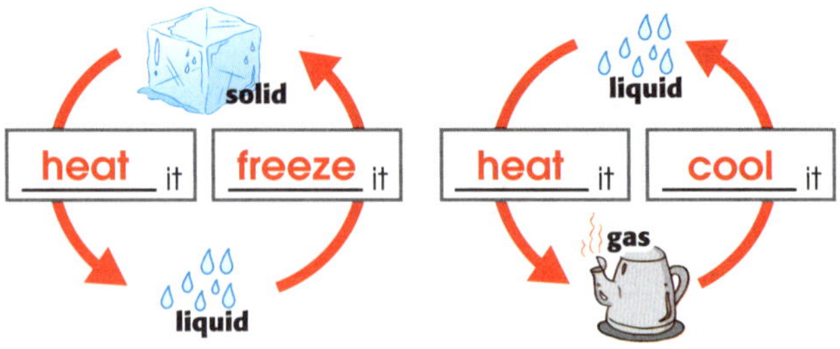

D. 1. ✔ ; gas
   2. ✔ ; solid
   3. ✔ ; solid
   4. ✔ ; liquid

E. 1. Glaciers
   2. rain
   3. Yes, they are forms of water. A glacier is a solid form of water and rain is its liquid form.

4 Water in the Environment

A. 1. rain ; L
   2. snow ; S
   3. hail ; S
   4. frost ; S

B.

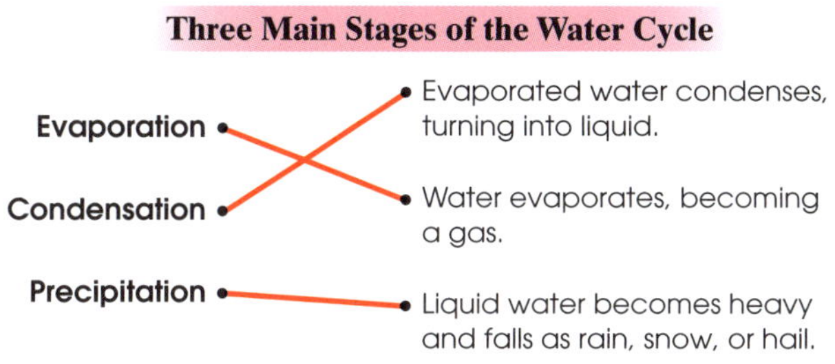

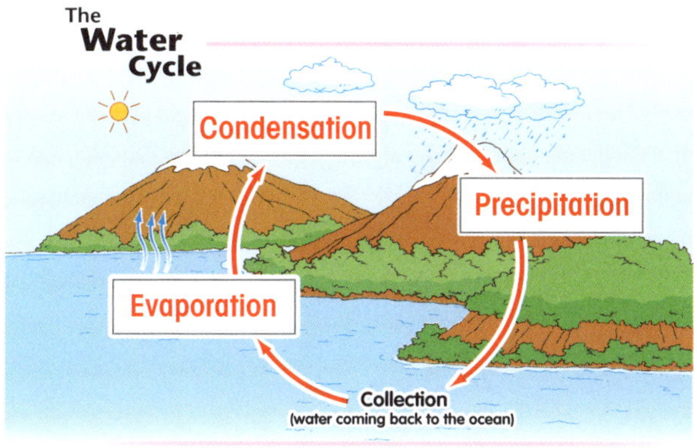

the sun

C. 1. condensation
   2. precipitation
   3. evaporation
   4. evaporation
   5. condensation

5 Water Sources and Uses

A. 1. well
   2. river
   3. lake
   4. fresh

B. 1. lake ; water treatment plant ; water supply system
   2. It filters, cleans, and treats the water. These functions are important because they make the water safe to drink.

C. Daily Activity: cooking ; bathing ; drinking ; mopping
   Transportation: ship ; submarine ; speedboat
   Appliance: air conditioner ; dishwasher ; washing machine
   Sports: swimming ; skiing
   Leisure: gardening ; making pottery

6 Air and Water Pollution

A. 1. B
   2. B
   3. A
   4. A

B. 1. Factories ; Follow
   2. Farming ; Use
   3. coal ; oil ; water
   4. car ; fuel spills ; public transit

C. 1. It is formed when polluted air mixes with water vapor.
   2. It can harm living things, including plants and fish.